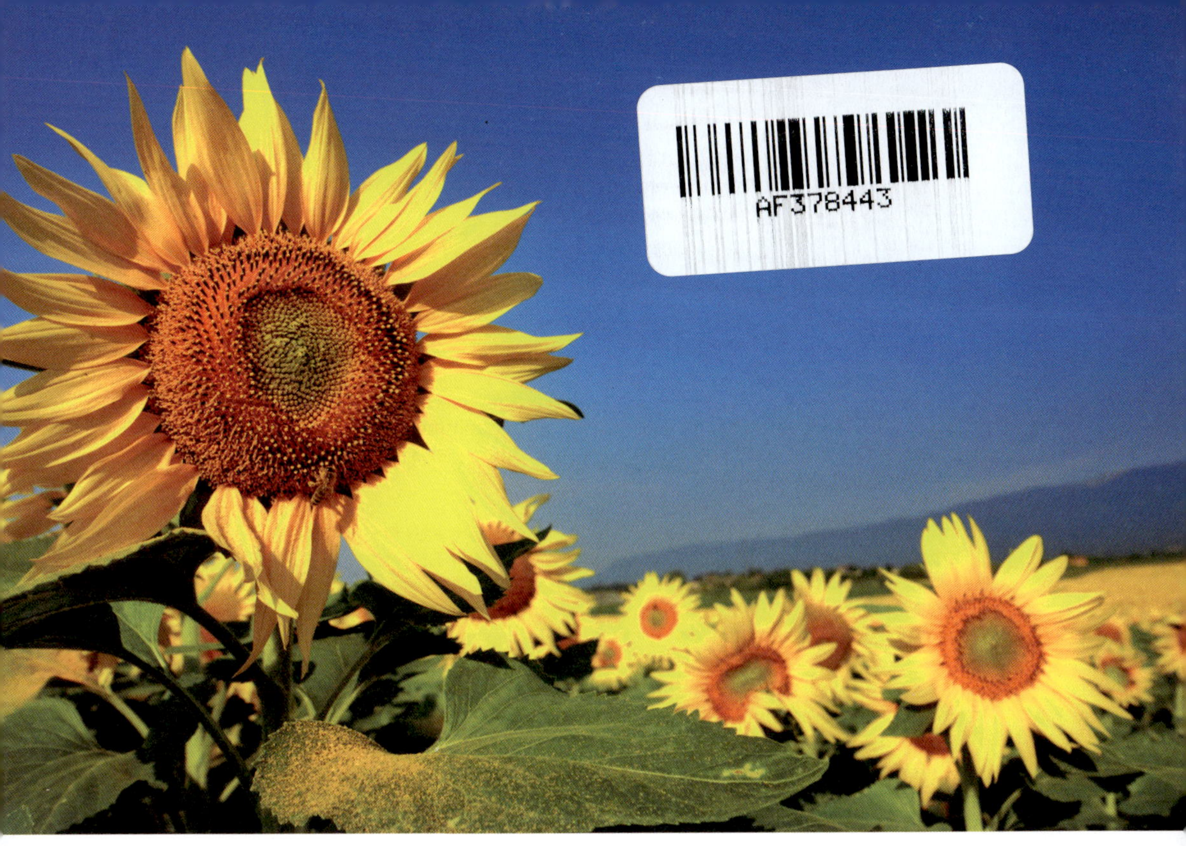

The Greatest Guide to

Photography

This is a **GREATEST**GUIDES title

Greatest Guides Limited, Woodstock, Bridge End, Warwick CV34 6PD, United Kingdom

www.greatestguides.com

Series created by Harshad Kotecha

All photographs © Alistair Scott except: P94 © Eric Gevaert; P96 © Gina Sanders; P118 © aliengel; P121 © Victor Pogontsev; P131 © Anatoly Tiplyashin; P132 © Kurhan; P134 © Darren Baker; P135 © Simone van den Berg; P136 © Jaimie Duplass; P138 © Monkey Business; P139 © Miroslava Arnaudova; P140 © Debbie0 (Fotolia), P89 © Wuka (iStockphoto), P122 © Tyler Olson (Dreamstime).

Every effort has been made to ensure that this book contains accurate and current information. However, neither the author nor the publisher shall be liable for any loss or damage suffered by readers as a result of any information contained herein.

All trademarks are acknowledged as belonging to their respective companies.

Greatest Guides is committed to a sustainable future for our planet. This book is printed on paper certified by the Forest Stewardship Council.

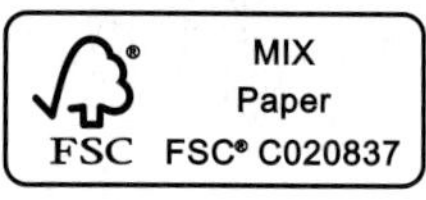

Printed and bound in the United Kingdom

ISBN 978-1-907906-10-7

For Chris, for Ros, and for Debs.

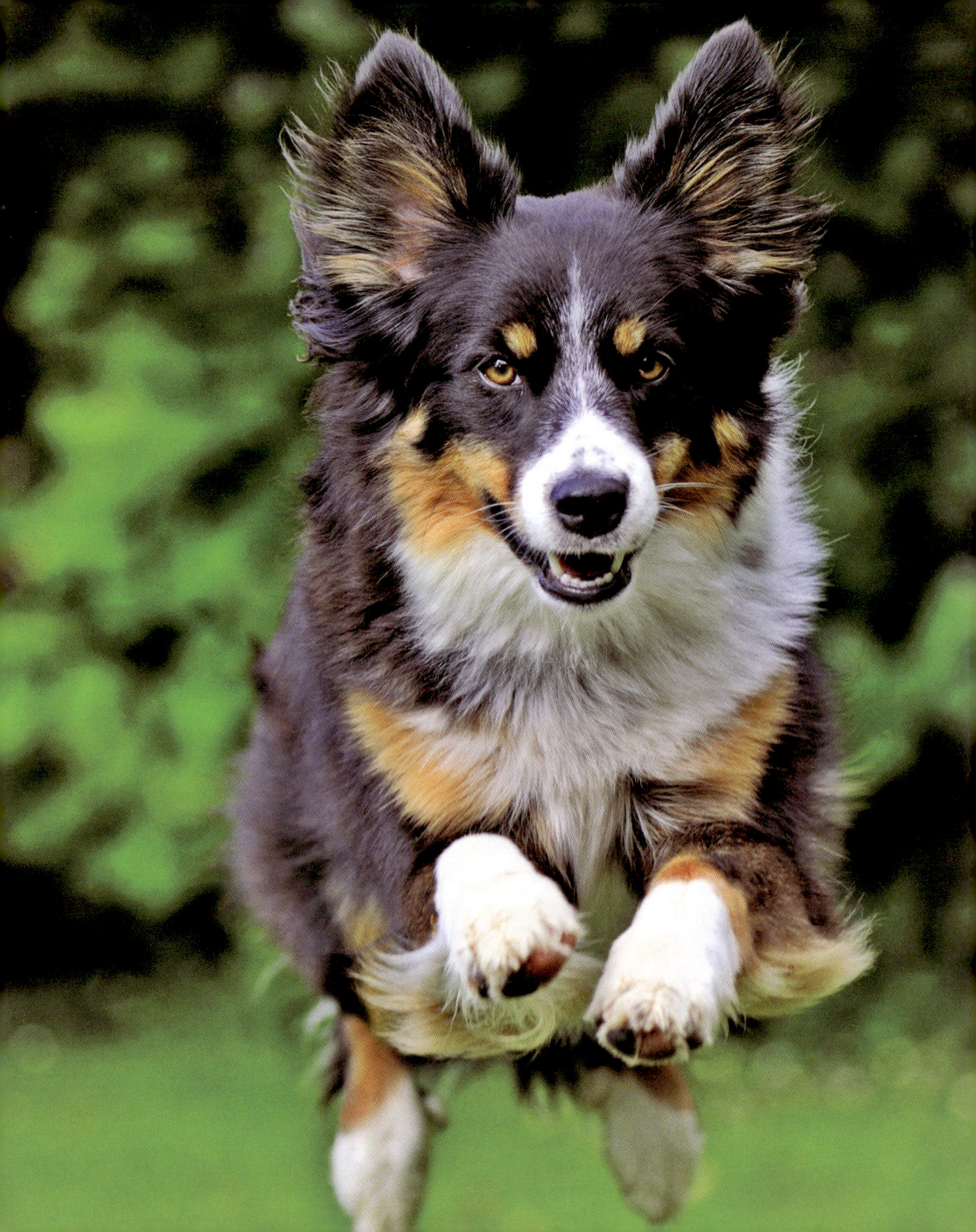

Contents

A few words from Alistair…

Almost everyone owns a camera, whether it's a little snapper tucked away inside a phone, a professional job with a lens like a howitzer, or one that still uses that good, old-fashioned film. And taking photographs is easy. You only have to push the button and a modern camera will do everything for you … exposure, shutter speed, focusing … it handles it all with electronic efficiency.

So, if your camera does it all, why do you need a book like this?

Because, just as all the bells and whistles of a word-processor won't turn a hack writer into a Shakespeare, so all the automation on your camera will not turn you into a better photographer. Cameras may be very sophisticated, but there is still nothing to equal the human brain for judging light conditions and the crucial moment; there is still nothing like the human eye for seeing shape and form.

In other words, it is the person behind the camera who matters. As the great landscape photographer Ansel Adams said, "You don't *take* a photograph. You *make* it." And that is still just as true today as it was when he said it.

'Making' good photographs is not difficult. But to do that you'll need to go a bit further than just raising your camera to your eye, pointing it and pressing the shutter button. You'll need to discover the best viewpoints, you may have to wait for the right light (or create it) and, if that light is difficult, you'll usually get a better photograph by over-riding the camera's automatic controls. Above all, you'll need to learn to 'see' rather than just 'look'.

The aim of this book is help you do all these things. In it I will cover everything from buying the best equipment, through composition and lighting, to making your photography pay. There are tips on portraiture and sports photography, hints on taking landscapes and even help with capturing a flash of lightning.

But there's one tip that is most important of all. Have fun! Get out and about with your camera, be creative, and come back with some stunning images that you can display in an album, frame for your wall, or even sell for a pleasant profit.

Enjoy your photography!

Alestair

"Photography is not a sport. It has no rules. Everything must be dared and tried!"

Bill Brandt

Kit and Caboodle

Chapter 1

Kit and Caboodle

Go into any camera shop and you'll be spoiled for choice … and beset by questions. Digital or film? Matchbox- or brick-sized? Six megapixels or twelve? Is 'face detection' worth having? What's the difference between 'vibration reduction' and 'image stabilization'? Is optical zoom better than digital zoom? And what is a megapixel, anyway?

Don't despair. When buying a camera there are some features that are essential, others that are useful, and a few that are not worth having. This chapter will cover the worthwhile and not-so worthwhile, and will also give ideas on some additional items that will help you get the best results with your photography.

But, before you begin, don't get too hung-up on your gear. Owning an expensive camera won't make you a good photographer any more than having an expensive stove will make you a good cook.

Consider the pioneers of photography. They used primitive and unwieldy equipment – glass photographic plates and magnesium flash powder. Their cameras were so huge and heavy that, if they were photographing landscapes, they needed mules to carry their gear. Some photographers even needed to take portable darkrooms with them. And yet they produced stunning images.

In photography, the crucial factor is the person behind the lens. You. Developing a good eye and learning to frame great scenes are far more important attributes than having a fancy camera.

Digital or film?

What if you have an old film camera? Is it still worth using it, or should you go digital?

This may seem like a no-brainer. Aren't all cameras digital these days? Film is out of date, isn't it?

Not necessarily. Be careful. Film is certainly not to be written off as something out of the Ark. Many professional photographers still use film cameras because they are more robust and can deliver images of the highest quality.

In addition, film cameras can be left switched on for much longer periods without draining the battery. This is ideal if you're into sports or wildlife photography. And, believe it or not, some film cameras don't even need a battery.

However, digital cameras do have advantages. They can be made a lot smaller and you see the results instantly. This means you can experiment … or re-take the family portrait when you accidentally caught little Freda picking her nose. Then you can print or e-mail your photos, or post them on websites.

This book is principally aimed at digital photographers, though the majority of the advice will apply to film users too.

P&S, Bridge or SLR?

There are three main groups of cameras, and each type has its advantages and disadvantages:

1. Compact cameras – also known as 'Point and Shoot' (P&S) – are pocketable cameras, ideal for capturing a shot at a moment's notice. The more sophisticated ones are packed with features such as 'intelligent exposure', touch screens and 'face detection'. Some even have a setting that will make your subjects look slimmer.

The main advantages of compact cameras are that they are small, lightweight and easy-to-use. They are popular with people who just want to take family shots, photos on vacations, at parties and similar. But this is not to say that you can't take other great photographs with them.

Their principal disadvantage is the small image sensor size. This means that they tend to produce lower-quality photographs (though you probably won't notice this unless you try to enlarge them), and they perform less well in dim light. Another disadvantage is that many compact cameras suffer from 'shutter lag' (see 'Don't be a Laggard', below). This can mean that you can miss shots in fast-moving situations.

2. System cameras – Also known as 'single lens reflex' (SLR, or DSLR for the digital versions). These are cameras with interchangeable lenses. They have the largest image sensors and so produce high-quality images that can be 'blown up' to poster size without any loss of quality.

    They are also more versatile. As their lenses are interchangeable, you can use all sorts of weird and wonderful ones – from extra wide-angles, that make it look as if you're photographing from inside a goldfish bowl, to ultra telephotos that let you get pictures of a lion's lunch … without becoming his dessert.

    Better still: if you already own a set of lenses for that camera brand (e.g. because you had one of their film cameras) they may well fit the digital model. But be careful. Because the sensor in a digital camera is not the same size as 35mm film, the zoom range will be different. Also, autofocus and exposure metering may not work with the old lenses.

    The disadvantages of system cameras are that they are expensive, bulky, and heavy, with fewer fully automatic features.

3. Bridge cameras. As their name suggests, these are half-way between compact and system cameras. They are larger than compacts and usually packed with features, but they do not have interchangeable lenses.

Their main advantages are that they have larger sensors than compacts, so giving a better quality of photograph, and they tend to have more versatile superzoom lenses. However, the fact that you can't change this lens, coupled with the higher price, are the principal disadvantages of bridge cameras.

Getting serious? Go single

What sort of camera is best?

That depends. If you're keen on photography and you're going to be taking landscape, wildlife, close-up, low-light or other specialized photographs, if you want to produce prints to hang on your wall, or if you want to sell your work, then you should think about going for a system camera.

On the other hand, if you just want to take photographs for the family album, to e-mail to friends or to post on your website, then a good-quality compact camera will produce these with the minimum of fuss.

Bridge cameras are best avoided as being neither one thing nor the other. Although they have more sophisticated features than compacts, the lack of an interchangeable lens is a handicap. You'll find that if you have a bridge camera, and you start getting serious about photography, you will rapidly run up against its limitations.

Good resolutions

The 'resolution' of a digital camera is a measure of the detail in the images it takes, and is measured in megapixels. A single 'pixel' (the name is shorthand for '*picture element*') is one tiny colored dot on a digital photograph. A 'megapixel' is simply a million of these.

At the heart of a digital camera is an electronic sensor that converts light into electrons. It is made of millions of tiny light-sensitive receivers packed into rows and columns. Each of these receivers collects the light for one pixel.

Sensors are rectangular, and the megapixel rating of a camera is calculated by multiplying the number of pixels along the long edge of the sensor by the number along the short side. It's exactly like working out the area of a rectangle at school (remember that?) except the answer is divided by a million to get a workable figure.

Prints charming

Salespeople and advertisements may try to tell you that the more megapixels you have in your camera the better.

This is not entirely true. The main importance of the megapixel rating is to tell you the maximum size of high-quality prints you can make.

How is this done? Simply divide the height and width of the sensor (in pixels) by the resolution of your desired print in pixels per inch (ppi).

For example, if you have a camera with a sensor that is 3008 by 2000 pixels (that's just over 6 megapixels), and you want to print photographs from it with a resolution of 300ppi (a standard resolution) then the biggest quality prints you can get are 10.0 × 6.6 inches (3008÷300 and 2000÷300).

You can, of course, make even larger prints. But the bigger you make them the poorer the quality will be.

The megapixel rating of a camera is certainly important. But it's definitely not the only feature you should consider when buying.

Size does matter

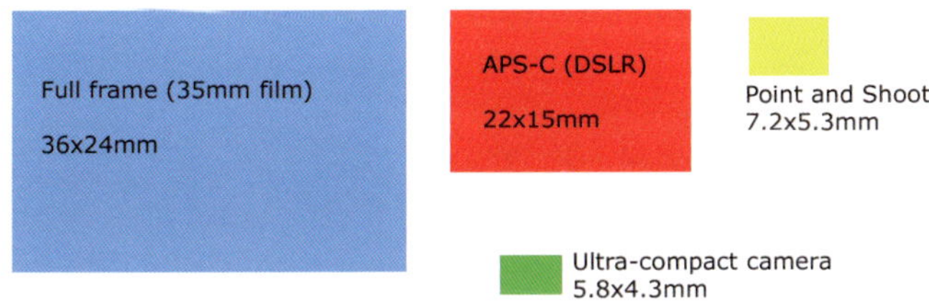

Packing in the pixels. Different sizes of camera sensor, drawn to scale.

An 8-megapixel camera from one maker may give a poorer-quality image than a 6-megapixel camera from another.

Why?

Because they use different-sized sensors.

The size of a camera's sensor is measured across the diagonal (like a television screen is) and sizes range from 9mm on a compact camera to 43mm on the professional models. That's about a 10 times difference in area.

It doesn't take a genius to work out that if you have a sensor with 8 million pixels, and it is 10 times smaller than one with 6 million, those 8 million are going to have to be seriously shrunk in order to fit them all in. As a result they become less efficient at gathering light. They may also be jammed together so tightly in the smaller sensor that they begin to interfere with each other, causing 'noise' (randomly colored specks, especially in darker areas).

So, 'the bigger the better' is definitely true with regard to sensor size.

Point of viewfinders

In the old days, photographers composed their images by peering through an optical viewfinder. Nowadays most people with digital cameras compose by looking at the little screen on the back. Manufacturers have spotted this and, in order to save space and make their cameras sleeker, some of them have done away with the optical viewfinder.

It is best to avoid buying a camera without a viewfinder. Why? Two reasons:

1. In bright sunlight it can be almost impossible to see the image on that little screen.

2. The digital screen drains battery power. Fast. You may be in a situation where something interesting is happening and your battery is running low. If your camera has a viewfinder you can switch off the screen to save power, and so keep shooting for longer.

Having a viewfinder on your camera allows you to keep your options open.

Holding your camera up to look through the viewfinder also helps to stabilize it.

Don't be a laggard

If you don't want to miss those never-to-be repeated photographs, like Freddy slamming home his first dunk shot, check the 'shutter lag' of a camera.

Most compact cameras have a brief delay of a few milliseconds before recording an image. This may not sound like a lot, but it can mean the difference between you capturing Freddy slamming the ball home … or just getting the empty basket.

So, if you are going to be taking action shots, go for a camera with little or no shutter lag. Or buy a system camera (they don't suffer from this).

Most automatic cameras set the exposure and focus as you press the shutter button. You can minimize shutter lag by getting this out of the way. Depress the shutter button half-way to let the camera do its measuring stuff, then hold it there, ready to fire when the action occurs.

Shooting in the raw

If you have a more advanced digital camera it may give you the option of taking JPEG or RAW files. What's the difference?

JPEG files are compressed so you can get more on your memory card. You can also take pictures more quickly as the smaller files don't take so long to save. In addition this is a standard format so files can be printed by any lab, e-mailed to family and friends or posted on a website.

On the other hand, RAW files are the raw data that is collected by the sensor. They are like a digital negative. And, like film negatives, they need further processing to turn them into viewable/printable files. You do this using an image editing program on your computer. RAW files are also much larger than JPEGs.

Extra processing? Larger files? Why would anyone want to use the RAW option?

The massive advantage of RAW files is that they give higher quality images. You probably won't be able to detect any difference on your computer screen, or even if you print photos for your album. But if you want to sell your photographs, or print them poster-sized, you should always take them in RAW format.

Please forgive me

Another huge advantage of RAW files is that if you make mistakes (who doesn't?) the format is more forgiving. For example, by using an image-editing program, an error such as under-exposure can be corrected in a RAW file much more successfully than it can in a JPEG one.

RAW files also retain the original data, no matter what you do to them. So you can always go back to the original, even if you have saved the file in between times. If you save changes to JPEG files (without re-naming the file) the original is gone.

You lose

Another disadvantage of JPEG is that it is a 'lossy' compression method. Information is discarded every time you save a file. This is usually not noticeable, but you should avoid saving and re-saving files (when processing, for example) as the image will be degraded a little each time.

You choose

So, which file type do you choose when you shoot? JPEG or RAW?

That depends on the size of your memory card, how much control you want over your images, and how much time you are able to spend working on them, later.

If you are going on holiday, just want to take pictures for the family album, and you have a limited memory storage, then stick with JPEG. You'll get more photos on your card, they'll be less work when you get home, and they will look perfectly good on screen, e-mailed or even printed.

On the other hand, if you are taking photographs to enlarge into posters, if you are going to try exhibiting them, entering for competitions, or if you want to sell them commercially, you'd better use RAW.

Raise your glass

The lens (known as 'glass' to the professionals) is the most important part of your camera. It is no use having the most expensive camera in the world if you're trying to take a picture through something that resembles the bottom of a beer bottle.

If you're buying a single lens reflex camera, it is always better to spend money on a superior lens rather than on a higher specification of camera body.

That's about the length of it

There are two measurements to consider when buying a lens – its focal length (or range of lengths, if it is a zoom lens), and maximum aperture.

The focal length (expressed in millimeters) is the magnification power of a lens. The longer the focal length of a lens the more it magnifies, and the smaller the area it covers.

The maximum aperture (expressed as an 'f number') is a measure of the amount of light a lens can gather. The lower the number, the more sensitive the lens. A lens with a maximum aperture of $f2$ will perform better in low light situations than a $f3.5$ lens.

Times tables

A lot of manufacturers express the power of a zoom lens as a multiplication figure, e.g. 10× zoom. This means that the focal length at maximum zoom is 10 times the focal length at the wide angle setting. However, it does not tell you the power of the telephoto.

Zoom-zoom

Some of the point and shoot cameras give two zoom figures – optical and digital. The digital zoom figure may make it sound as if the camera can take pictures of an elephant's eyelashes from a hundred paces.

Ignore it.

Digital zoom works by electronically enlarging a portion of the image already captured. In other words, it makes the pixels bigger, resulting in a poor quality, blocky-looking photograph. Optical zoom gives far higher quality because the lens enlarges the image before it is recorded.

In your prime

Although zoom lenses are standard on most cameras nowadays, it is still possible to buy fixed focal length ones (called 'prime lenses') for cameras with interchangeable lenses.

Why bother? Aren't zoom lenses much more convenient and versatile?

They are. But prime lenses are easier to design and manufacture. As a result they are usually cheaper, whilst giving a cracking optical performance. They also tend to be smaller and lighter, with a wider aperture than their zoom counterparts.

So, if you anticipate regularly using a 70-300mm telephoto lens at its maximum of 300mm (photographing wildlife, for example), think about buying a fixed 300mm lens instead. You will get a much better lens for your money.

Who needs a hood?

A lens hood is a conical tube, made of rubber or plastic, that fits on the front of the lens. Some cynics think that it's used to make the lens look bigger and more impressive.

And, you know what? It does make the lens look more impressive. But it has two much more important functions.

First, a lens hood keeps stray light off the surface of the lens which can lead to haze, lens flare and a loss of contrast. Second, it helps protect the important bits if you drop or knock your lens.

Use a lens hood … and ignore what the cynics think.

QUICK T!P

If you don't have a lens hood and you're shooting into the light, shade the front element of the lens with your hand or a hat. It doesn't look so impressive, but it works just as well.

To cap it all

When you buy a new interchangeable lens it will have little plastic caps fitted over each end. Don't throw them away! Keep the outer lens cap on the front of the lens whenever you are not taking photos. Use the inner one when you take the lens off the camera, as you will do when you get more and more lenses. You should also keep the cap that seals the body of a single-lens-reflex camera.

Filtered, anyone?

Will your camera lenses take filters? You can check by looking at the front of the mount to see if there is a screw thread incorporated into the narrow flange that sticks out forwards from the front. Most DSLR cameras have lenses that will take filters.

A filter is a piece of high-quality optical glass that alters the light entering the camera. There are filters for all sorts of purposes including changing the color of a scene, reducing light levels, darkening skies, or cutting haze.

QUICK T!P

If you want to use filters, ensure you buy high-quality ones. They may seem staggeringly expensive for what they are, but remember that you are putting an extra piece of glass in front of your lens, so it needs to be of the highest quality.

Now, forget the technology. Your camera is only a tool for your eyes and brain …

DID YOU KNOW …

The first successful photograph was taken in 1827 by Joseph Nicephore Niépce. It was a view from the window of his country house in France. The shutter speed was 8 hours and the 'film' was a pewter plate.

The first practical photographic process was invented by Louis Daguerre, and called the Daguerreotype. It was discovered by accident in 1835 and announced to the public in 1839. The French government bought the rights to it in the same year.

The first Daguerrotypes required shutter speeds of 10 to 20 minutes. So, if you wanted your portrait taken you had to sit very still. Head clamps were used to hold people still for that length of time.

The first photographs were all monochrome. If photographers wanted color prints the color had to be applied by hand, using a fine paintbrush.

Chapter summary

- Decide if you want to buy a 'point and shoot' or a DSLR.

- Avoid ' bridge cameras' They are neither one thing nor the other.

- If you buy a DSLR with interchangeable lenses, go for the best lens you can afford.

- A prime lens may give better results than a zoom.

- Use a lens hood whenever you can.

- Before you buy a 'point and shoot', check its shutter lag.

- Sensor size is more important than megapixels. The larger the sensor the better.

- Ignore digital zoom ratings.

- Shoot in RAW mode for the best quality and most flexibility.

- Filters can enhance colors, reduce light levels and cut haze.

> **"***A photograph is a secret about a secret. The more it tells you the less you know.***"**

Diane Arbus

How to be a Sharpshooter

Chapter 2

How to be a Sharpshooter

Clear, crisp, well-focused pictures are the aim of most photographers … most of the time. Nothing ruins a photograph more than unintentional fuzziness. So look closely at your photos and be critical with yourself. Are you getting shark-tooth-sharp ones? Maybe they look great on your monitor, but that will probably be displaying them at a resolution of only 72 pixels per inch (ppi), which is very forgiving. When you enlarge them you could be in for a disappointment.

Here are some tips to help you get sharp pictures or, sometimes, a touch of controlled blur.

Hold on

Cameras are now so small and lightweight that you may be tempted to shoot one-handed. You can sometimes see this being done in camera adverts, where a 'cool' photographer leans out of a sports car, jives at a party, or dangles from a cliff face, shooting one-handed.

That's a laugh. No serious photographer ever does that if it can be avoided.

You should only use one hand in the most extreme circumstances – if you are trapped in a crowd, for example, and the only way to get a shot is to hold the camera high over your head. At all other times, use both hands, one supporting the camera body, the other around the lens. And tuck your elbows in to your sides. No matter how calm and relaxed you are, your hands are going to shake a little. By using both at the same time, you help cancel out these slight tremors.

Ah, but I don't need to worry about the shakes …

… I've got image stabilization on my camera.

Congratulations. An image stabilization (IS) feature will certainly help improve the sharpness of your images. On other cameras it may be called vibration reduction (VR). They're the same, and they allow you to use a slower shutter speeds in a given setting. But don't rely on them. Whether you have IS or VR, you still cannot defy the laws of physics. In photography it is best to get the fundamental techniques well established. Then everything else is a bonus.

But don't hold your breath

In some photographic guides you may read the advice to hold your breath when pushing the shutter button in order to minimize vibrations still further.

Don't bother. Holding your breath is not a natural action, and you are likely to be shaking even more … or suffocating.

Continue to breathe in and out slowly and naturally and, if you're not shooting fast action, try to press the shutter release at the moment when you've fully exhaled.

Just adjust

Many camera viewfinders have a little adjuster which allows you to compensate for your vision. The first thing to do when you buy a new camera is to set this to match your viewfinder eye. And check it from time to time, too. Your eyesight may change, or the adjuster may get knocked out of place. You cannot hope to get sharp photographs if you cannot see the scene correctly in the first place.

Let's get this in focus

Most cameras have some form of auto-focus. This one feature that professionals regularly use. But, good though it is, you can't always rely on it. When the autofocus is switched on, your camera may not allow you to take a picture unless it thinks the image is in focus. This means that in fast-changing situations, such as photographing children, sports, or parades, you can miss shots while the camera tries to focus.

If the autofocus is stopping you from taking photographs because it is reacting too slowly, there are two ways to deal with it:

1. In predictable situations, such as in certain sports where the action is going to take place in one small area, switch the autofocus off, manually focus on the 'action area' and wait. Much of what you watch through the viewfinder may be out of focus, but when something does happen and you shoot, you're more likely to capture a sharp image.

2. In unpredictable situations, such as photographing children, you can improve your chances of getting a sharp shot by using something called 'depth of field'.

Now … don't panic … this is going to require a teeny bit of theory …

How deep is my field?

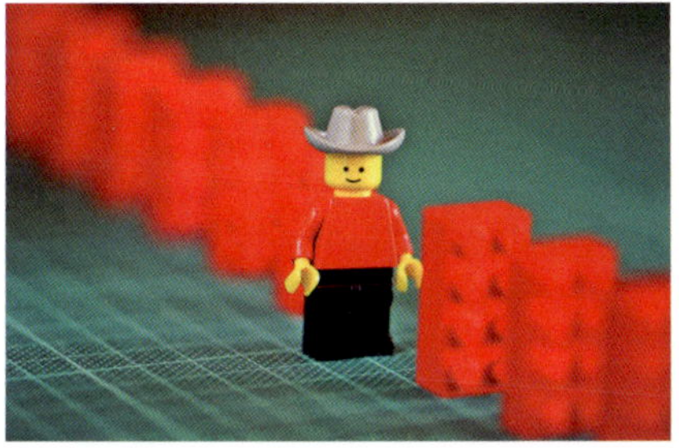

The lens aperture, wide open at $f2.8$, gives a shallow depth of field.

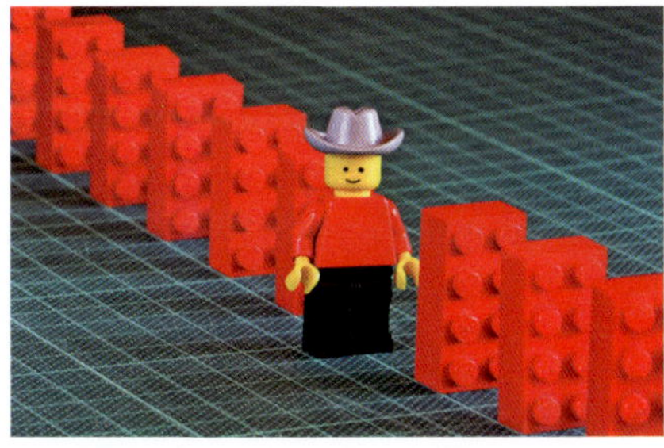

The depth of field is much broader when the aperture is closed down to $f22$.

Useful fact – when a camera lens is focused on a particular point, the image is acceptably sharp for a short distance in front of, and behind that point.

For example, if little Freda is sitting still for a portrait, and you've focused on her eyes, the tip of her nose may also be in focus, and her ears too. That range, front to back, is called the 'depth of field' (DOF).

The depth of field in any situation depends on the focal length of the lens (telephoto lenses tend to have a smaller depth of field) and – very important – the aperture. The smaller the aperture the greater the depth of field.

A depth of field scale may be marked on your lens. It's those mysterious figures on either side of the central focus mark. If they are not marked then you can find DOF calculators online (a useful resource is given in the appendix) or photographic shops sell inexpensive cards giving the details.

Getting hyper …

So … now you know about depth of field. How does that help you focus on little Freda, who's now racketing round like a banshee?

It's simple. Set your lens to its hyperfocal distance – that is, the point where everything from half that distance to infinity is in focus.

Obviously this varies according to the aperture, but it's easy to find if you have a depth of field scale on your lens. Simply rotate the focus until the infinity mark (∞) is aligned with the mark indicating the aperture you have set. Then it's done. Everything from half that distance to infinity will be in focus and you've a good chance of getting a sharp shot of little Freda.

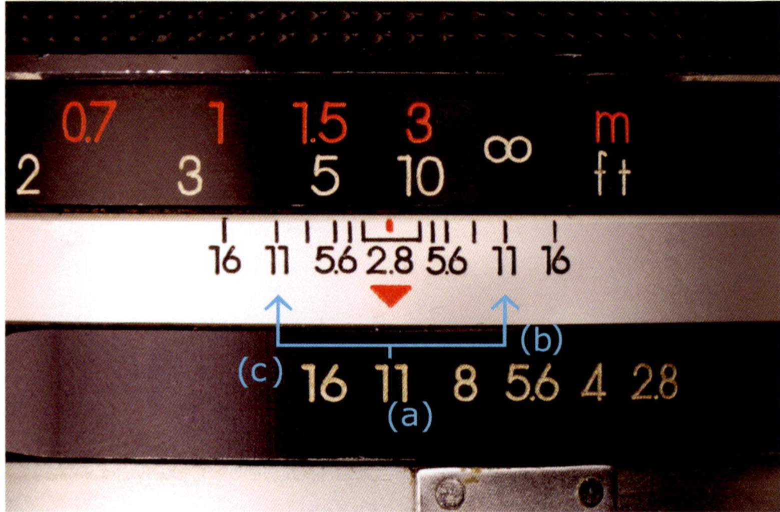

Hyperfocal distance. With the aperture set to ƒ11 (a) and the infinity focus mark against ƒ11 on the depth of field scale (b) the lens will be in focus all the way down to about 1.3 meters (c).

Unfortunately, most lens manufacturers have stopped engraving a depth of field scale on their lenses. Some lenses don't even have distance markings for focusing any more. But, despite these limitations, you can still use the hyperfocal distance. You just have to estimate. Here's how to do it:

There may be a DOF calculator in the back of the instruction booklet for your lens. Or you can find DOF calculators online (see appendix). Use one of these to find the hyperfocal distance for the focal length and aperture you will be using. Then pre-focus on a nearby object that you estimate is at the hyperfocal distance and – voilà! – it's done.

QUICK T!P

If your camera's autofocus is a bit slow, it's a good idea, when carrying your camera, to have it switched off and the lens permanently set to its hyperfocal distance. Then you are instantly ready to take an in-focus photo in any unexpected situation.

Shake it up baby now!

You know your focus is spot on, yet your photo is still blurry. What's happened?

You've probably got camera shake. In other words, the shutter speed was too slow for hand-holding, even if you *were* using both hands.

If you want sharp images the 'rule of thumb' for hand-holding is to ensure shutter speed is higher than the focal length of the lens. For example, if your lens is set to 100mm focal length then use a shutter speed of 1/100th second, or higher.

However, to be really sure of pin-sharp images, use a shutter speed that is over three times the focal length, i.e. in the example above, 1/300th second or more.

QUICK T!P

If you can't use a high enough shutter speed because of dim light, then try bracing the camera against a lamp-post, wall, or some other solid object.

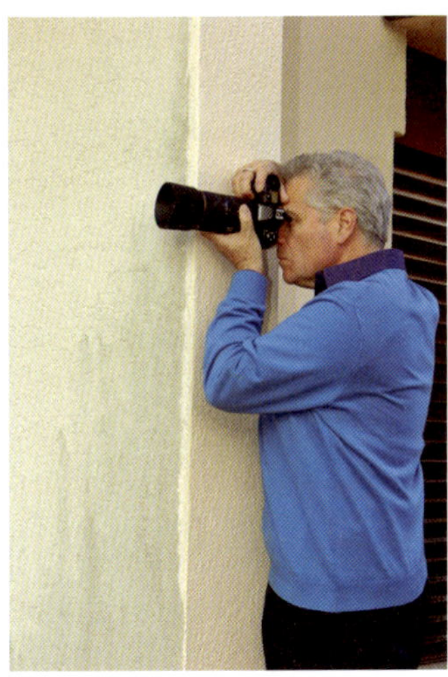

If you have no tripod, bracing your camera against a solid object can help keep it steady. And a bean bag will help cushion the camera.

Two legs good – three legs better

To eliminate camera shake entirely, use a tripod.

A tripod is one of the most valuable accessories you can buy. In fact, some professional photographers say that the first thing you should do after you've bought a camera is to weld it to a tripod.

Maybe that's going a bit far; but tripods are essential for taking pictures in low-light situations such as building interiors, nightscapes, or dawn landscapes, and when using telephoto lenses.

And there is another advantage. A tripod slows you down. Yes … that's right. It makes you look at elements of a picture such as composition and lighting.

Over-extended

When using the tripod, don't extend the legs, or the center column further than you need. The more they are extended, the less steady the set-up. Bring them out only enough to enable you to get your camera into the correct position. And switch image stabilization off. For some reason the mechanism is fooled by the camera being perfectly still.

Downhill all the way

If you're using a tripod on a steep slope, make sure you place one of its legs facing directly downhill. The tripod is more stable that way.

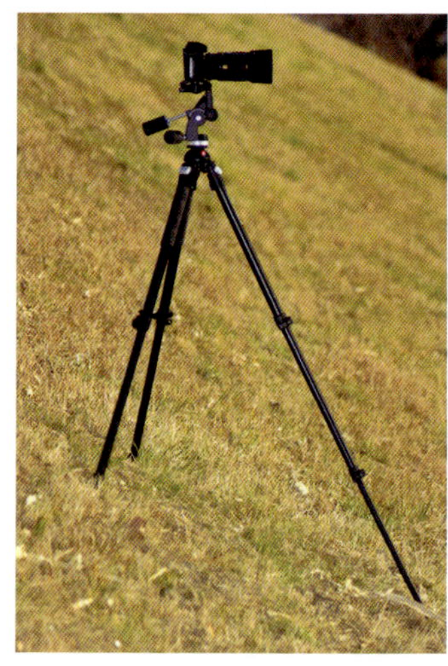

When using your tripod on a slope keep one leg pointing directly downhill for stability.

When quick doesn't click

Many tripods have a built-in quick-release mechanism. You screw your camera to a little plate and it snaps on and off your tripod in a jiffy. This enables you to switch quickly from hand-holding to tripod use, and back again.

But take care! More photographic gear has been broken through these things quick-releasing of their own accord than for any other reason. Make sure the mechanism is secure before you let it take the full weight of your camera.

One leg works too

If you're traveling light, want to move around a lot, or are working in a crowded setting where a tripod would cause an obstruction, you can use a monopod. Many professional sports photographers use them to help stabilize their massive lenses. They don't work as well as tripods, but they give you much more flexibility, take up very little space and are highly maneuverable.

What's more, you can often get away with using a monopod in places where setting up a tripod would bring officials down on you – inside buildings for example.

QUICK T!P

A monopod is also great for taking overhead photographs. Fix your camera to it, set the lens to wide angle, hold it high and use a remote release (see below) or the self-timer to fire the shutter. You can get some unusual views this way and, if you're stuck in a crowd, completely clear shots of the action. Things may be a bit crooked in the final image (though usually less than you'd imagine) but you can straighten them up with an image editor, anyway.

Full of beans

If you can't use a tripod or a monopod – if you're in the car taking wildlife shots, for example – use a beanbag to support your camera against the door frame. A beanbag takes up very little space, and you can also use it to brace against walls, lamp-posts or any other solid object.

Best of all, when you are traveling carry the bag empty and fill it up with beans, rice, dry sand, etc., when you reach your destination.

Don't try to use your beanbag in a car if the engine is running. You'll get more vibrations than you started with!

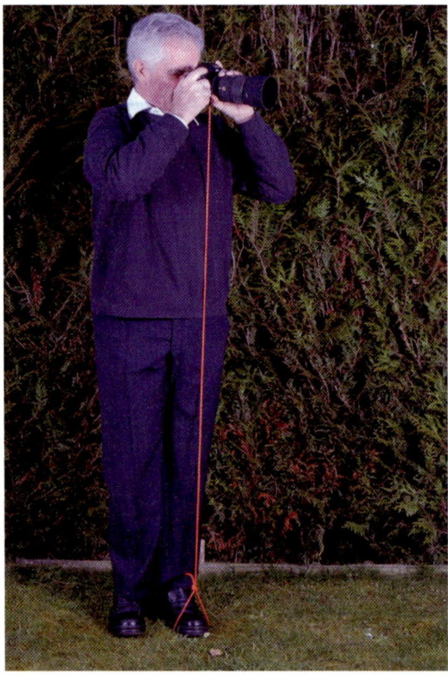

How to use your stringpod. Just don't pull too hard.

Make yourself a stringpod

Here's another cunning little gadget that you can make to help reduce camera shake at slower shutter speeds. It's called a stringpod, costs next to nothing and fits in a pocket.

Find a bolt that fits into your tripod socket (1/4"-20 is the standard size. That means 1/4" bolt with 20 threads per inch). Better still, find a 1/4" eyebolt. Take a long piece of strong string, or thin rope, and tie it to the bolt. Then tie a loop at the far end so that, when the bolt is screwed into the tripod socket, and you are holding the camera to your eye, you can put your foot in the loop and pull the string tight.

That's all you have to do. Use it when you haven't got your tripod or monopod, and when there's nothing suitable to rest your camera on. But don't pull too hard or you will be shaking with the effort. Pulling just hard enough to provide some tension should steady the camera significantly.

Remote control

If you want to cut vibrations to an absolute minimum when your camera is on a tripod, use a remote release (sometimes called a cable release). This is a cord that fits into a special socket on your camera and enables you to operate it from a distance. Just be sure to wait a few seconds for the vibrations to settle before firing the shutter.

Timing to perfection

If you haven't got a remote release, another way to cut vibrations is to use the self-timer on your camera. Set it for a good few seconds (15 should do) press the shutter button, and step back. By the time the shutter fires any vibrations that you have caused should have died away.

Lock 'em up

In an SLR vibrations can still be created by the internal mirror, which merrily slaps up and down as you take the picture … even if you are using a tripod with a cable release (or the self-timer).

Some SLRs have a facility called 'mirror lock-up' which sets the mirror in the raised position. Unfortunately you won't be able to see anything through the viewfinder when you use it, so it's only suitable for static subjects such as landscapes. Compose your picture first, then raise the mirror to cut vibrations to an absolute minimum, and take the photo.

Winded?

Another source of vibrations can be the wind, whistling around your set-up.

To overcome this, hang a heavy object from the center of the tripod to damp down the vibrations. Your backpack will do the job nicely. But don't make it too heavy. You don't want the tripod to collapse under the weight.

Or, if you've made yourself a stringpod (see above), you can use that. Tie it to the center column of your tripod so that the foot loop just touches the ground, put your foot in the loop and gently press down.

It's the law

Your camera is firmly fixed to a tripod, with your backpack hanging from it to damp down any vibrations, you've focused perfectly, locked the mirror up and you're using a remote release. Now there is just one more thing to do to ensure maximum sharpness. Set your lens aperture to its mid-range (usually ƒ5.6 to ƒ8).

There's no mystery in this. Because of the Laws of Physics (which we don't need to go into here) lenses perform best at mid-apertures. Look at the results of any lens test and you will see this. The optimum aperture setting is often called the 'sweet spot'. Try to find the 'sweet spot' of your lens by experimenting, or reading the equipment reviews, and use it whenever you can.

Sharp and sharper

Why all this concern with taking sharp photographs? There's probably a tool called 'sharpening' in your image editing program. Can't you use that to correct any blurriness?

No. That's like trying to correct a badly-cooked meal by adding ingredients after you've taken it out of the oven. Sure, a dash of sauce will add the finishing touches to a perfect dish. But no amount of sauce … or anything else … will transform bad cooking into *haute cuisine*. Similarly, there is no substitute for getting your photographs perfectly focused and shake-free when you take them.

Poetry in motion

Sometimes you want a little blur to indicate rapid movement, particularly in the background. For example, if you are taking photos of little Freda riding her bike round the garden, using a slightly slower shutter speed will blur the rotation of the wheels, her feet on the pedals, and the shrubs behind. All this will give an impression of speed.

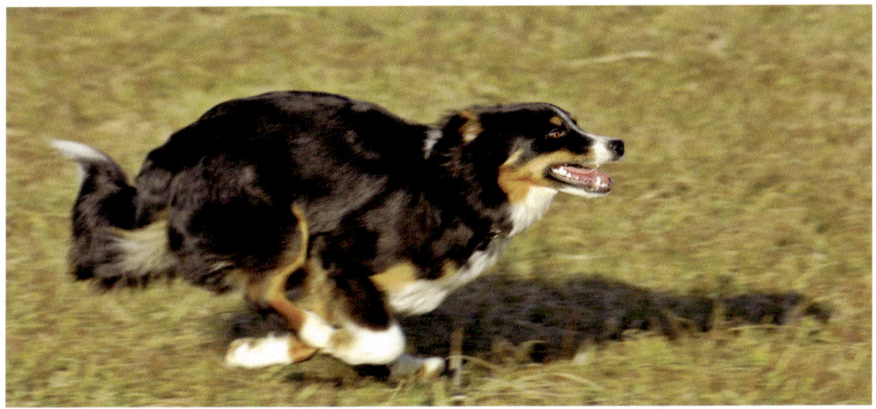

Aim for the eyes. Keep them in sharp focus.

Just be sure to get at least one thing sharp, preferably her face. There is little value in images that are blurred throughout. They just look like mistakes.

Last resort

One day you may find yourself faced with a unique photographic opportunity when the light is failing, you've got the camera turned up to its maximum sensitivity and you can only hand-hold. You're going to suffer from camera shake, whatever you do. But there's a simple way of getting the sharpest image possible.

Switch your camera to take JPEG images in burst mode. Focus on the scene, brace your camera as well as you can and hold your finger down on the shutter button. As you fire away you will be shaking to various degrees. Some of your images are going to be sharper than others.

Later, when you've downloaded the images on to your computer, look at the file sizes and pick the largest one. That should be the sharpest. The theory behind this is that the larger the file size (for closely similar photos) the sharper the images, because they have been compressed less.

Note: *This is not a way of eliminating the shakes*. It is simply a way of finding the picture with the least blur. Of course, ideally you should always use a tripod and have plenty of light. But sometimes you can't, and this technique may work as a last resort.

DID YOU KNOW ...

Disposable and automatic cameras aren't so new. In 1888 the Kodak company revolutionized photography by offering a camera that could be operated by a single button. Once the 100 pictures in it were taken, you sent the whole thing back. Kodak would then develop the film, reload your camera, and return prints and camera.

The word 'Kodak' was invented by George Eastman. He chose a strong, incisive letter – 'K' – and tried lots of combinations of letters that made words starting and ending with it. The fact that the word sounds like the clicking of a shutter may have helped its success.

The longest-lived camera brand is the Kodak Brownie. From the first cardboard and wood model in 1900 to the compact molded plastic cartridge loading pocket camera in 1980, almost 100 models bore the famous name. Many famous photographers have said that their interest began with a Brownie box camera.

Chapter summary

- Hold your camera with both hands.

- Don't hold your breath. Breathe evenly, to minimize camera shake.

- Use a tripod, monopod or a bean bag, whenever you can.

- Hang a weight from your tripod to reduce vibrations from the wind.

- Use mirror lock-up and either the self-timer or remote control to reduce vibrations.

- Close the aperture of your lens for greatest depth of field.

- Keep your lens set to its hyperfocal distance for grab-shots.

- Know the aperture 'sweet spot' of your lens, and use it whenever possible.

- If you are hand-holding, use a shutter speed that is higher than the focal length of the lens (e.g. 100mm lens – shutter speed faster than 1/100th second).

- Use motion blur creatively, to indicate speed.

- Get your photographs right in the camera.

"*Everything has its beauty. But not everyone sees it.*"

Confucius

Compose Yourself

Chapter 3

Compose Yourself

Whenever you look through the viewfinder of your camera you're composing a picture. You're deciding 'I want a picture of *this*'.

The danger is, we often concentrate on *this*, someone's face for example, and fail to see other elements such as what's going on in the background, the foreground or the corners. The camera doesn't. It 'sees' everything, in exactly the same way as a tape recording of conversation also picks up all the surrounding creaks, thuds and traffic noises.

Although your camera only captures a small rectangle of a scene, it's amazing how much junk can creep into that space. This is where the good photographer takes control, deciding what to include and what to leave out, choosing an angle, view and settings that emphasize the subject whilst minimizing any elements that distract from it.

There are certain rules that can help you. This chapter will cover them … but it will also suggest that you can break them sometimes, too.

Kiss

Every good photograph has a 'subject' … the reason why you pointed your camera in that direction in the first place. One of the cardinal rules of composition is 'KISS' – 'Keep It Simple, Stupid'. The more irrelevant things you have in a picture the more 'lost' your subject will be.

At the extreme, notice how many commercial photographs are nothing but the subject, with a plain background, usually white.

Opposite: Shooting your subjects against a pure white background is difficult, but it will make them stand out.

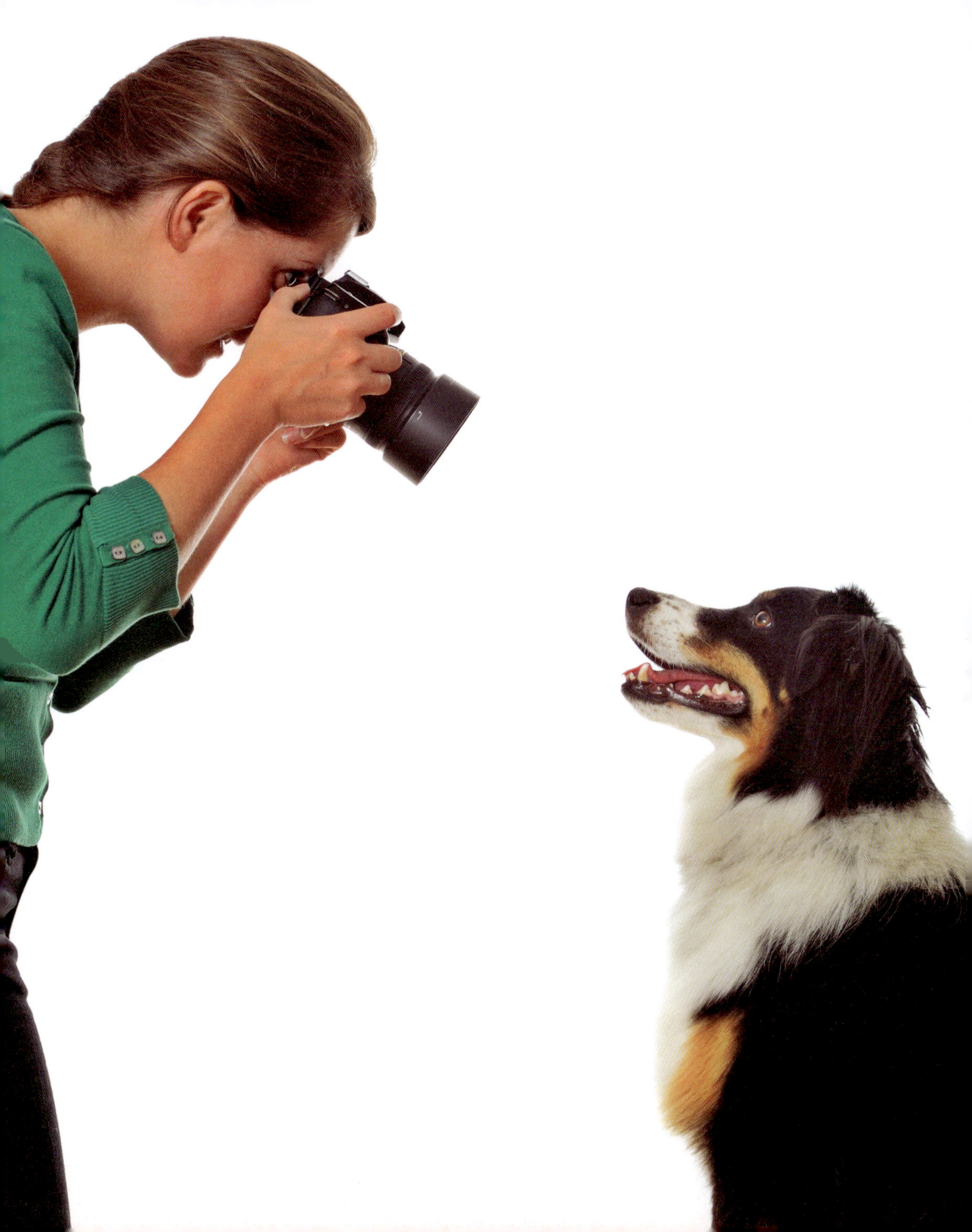

Try it sideways

It's amazing how many photographers don't ever think to turn their camera sideways, to get a vertical shot. This is the simplest-ever composition technique, and it is ideally suited for certain subjects, e.g. a full-length portrait of someone.

On top of that, if you are hoping to sell your photographs (see later) the vertical format is much more suitable for the covers of magazines and brochures.

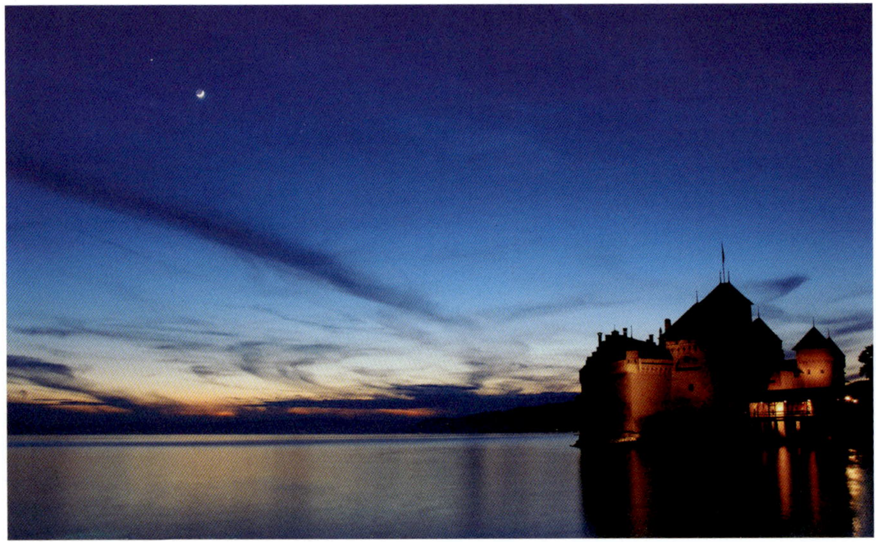

Above: Most photographs are taken in horizontal (landscape) format because that's the way that cameras are arranged.

Opposite: But turning your camera through 90 degrees can change the 'feel of a photograph, and some images are more suited to this format.

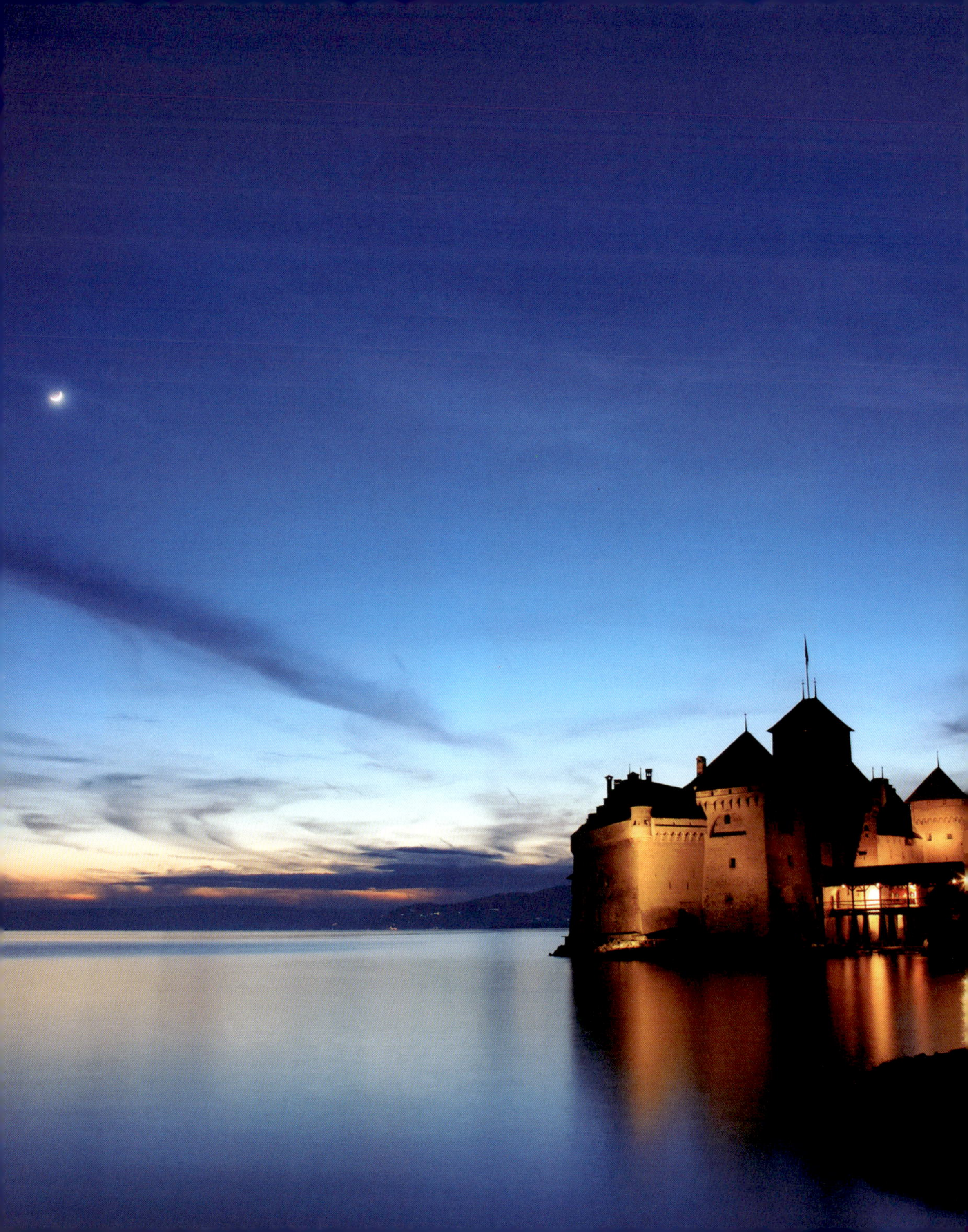

Background material

Objects like utility poles, lamp-posts and overhead wires adore being photographed. They have a habit of sneaking into photos, often placing themselves so that they appear to be growing out of someone's head. So, look at the background before you press the shutter, and move position to keep these intruders out. If you are taking a group portrait, for example, try standing your subjects against a thick hedge, or plain wall.

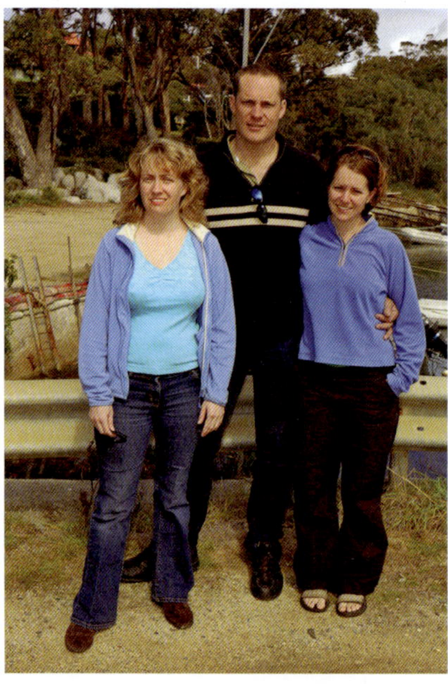

The background is very 'busy' with assorted junk, and there is a pole growing out of the man's head.

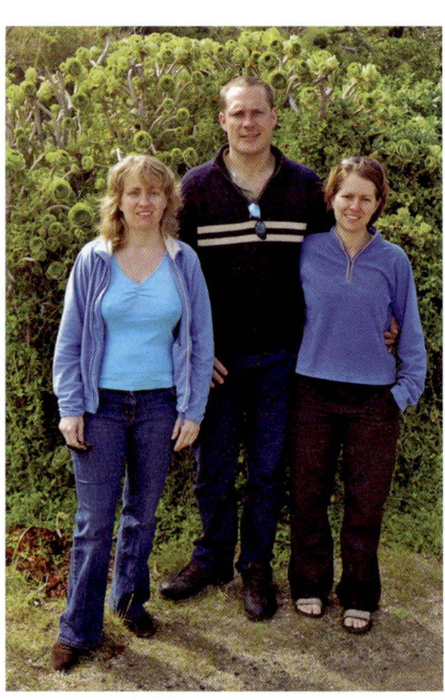

Finding a new, neutral background may require nothing more than turning around.

Don't get cornered

Be sure to look down in the corners, too, to check that no discarded candy wrappers, soft drinks bottles or other garbage has crept in. Yes, these things can be erased with image editing programs, but it's easier to remove them at the time. Once again … get it right in the camera.

It's a frame-up

A good foreground can add to an image, providing context and leading the viewer's eye into the picture.

One of the most effective ways of doing this is to choose a spot where your subject is surrounded by natural-looking objects. For example, if you are taking a picture of a church, choose a spot where it is framed by trees.

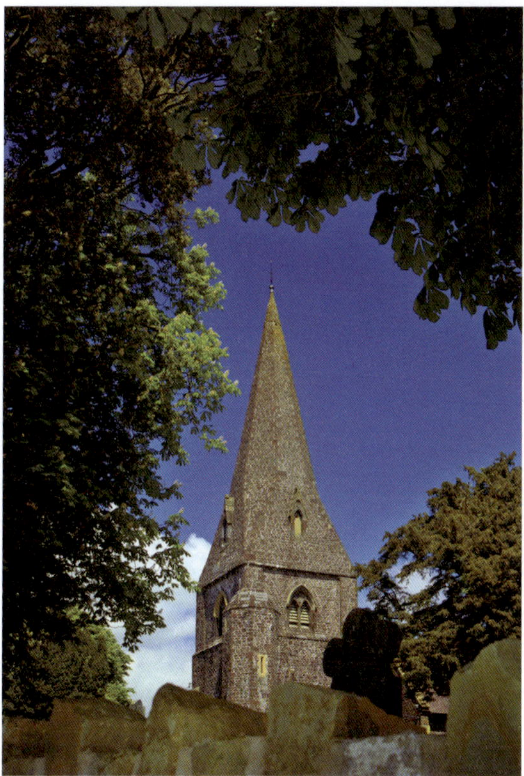

The tree frames the church spire. But maybe the frame is a bit too heavy in this case.

Many things can be used as frames for your subject including archways, windows, doors, narrow alleyways or rock formations.

QUICK T!P

Try to avoid having your 'frame' on only one side of the photograph as this tends to make it look off-balance.

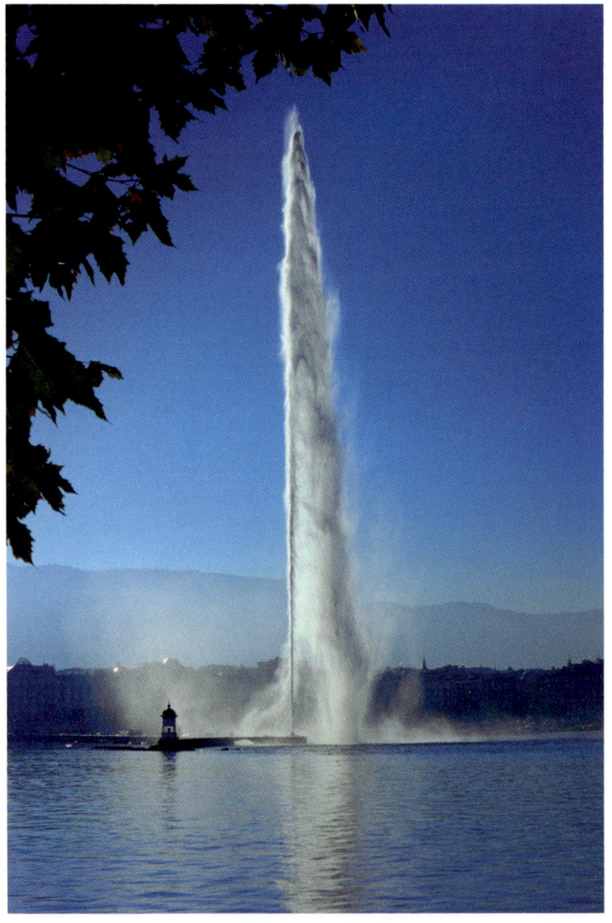

Try to avoid creating an unbalanced frame.

Anyone for tick-tac-toe?

Imagine drawing a tick-tac-toe grid on a scene in your viewfinder, so that it's divided it into thirds horizontally and vertically.

Artists have long known that pictures look more pleasing and dynamic if prominent lines (such as the horizon, tops of walls, or the sides of buildings) lie along one or other of these lines. Similarly, points of interest (such as a figure, or a tree) tend to look better if they are positioned at the intersections. This is called the 'Rule of Thirds'.

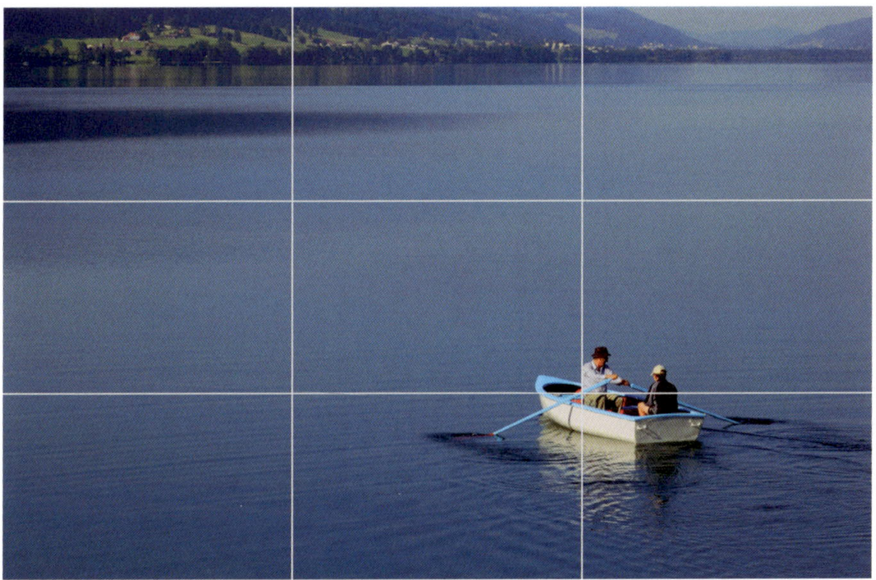

Dividing your image in to three, horizontally and vertically, and placing your subject at an intersection, gives a classic composition.

QUICK T!P

Some cameras have a grid of these lines in the viewfinder that can be switched on and off. Use it to help you compose.

Have you got center spot syndrome?

Don't worry. There's no need to go to the doctor. It's that autofocus spot, in the middle of your viewfinder that can cause the trouble. You home in on your subject with it, focus, and then shoot.

And what do you get? Your subject slap-bang in the center of the photo. Every time. There's nothing wrong with that except that it gives boring, repetitive compositions.

But, if you don't place that spot on to your subject, how do you focus? Easy. Most cameras have a two stage shutter release. Press it a little way and the lens will focus, press it further and the picture is taken. So … focus on your subject with a gentle push, hold the button down while you recompose, then press the shutter all the way. Yes, it is a bit more trouble, but it will get more interesting and varied photographs.

Try angles

Ask any engineer – a triangle is the strongest shape in construction. You can see them in pylons, bridges, bicycle frames, everywhere. And triangles are pretty strong in photography too. They can be formed by obvious lines, or by objects at each corner of a virtual one. Look for them in different places – for example, railway tracks disappearing into the distance, three boats on a lake, or birds. Include them, and your pictures will be stronger.

QUICK T!P

Don't forget squares, rectangles, circles and ellipses. They may not be as strong as a triangle, but they still give good compositions in photographs.

Opposite: Triangles provide a strong compositional element.

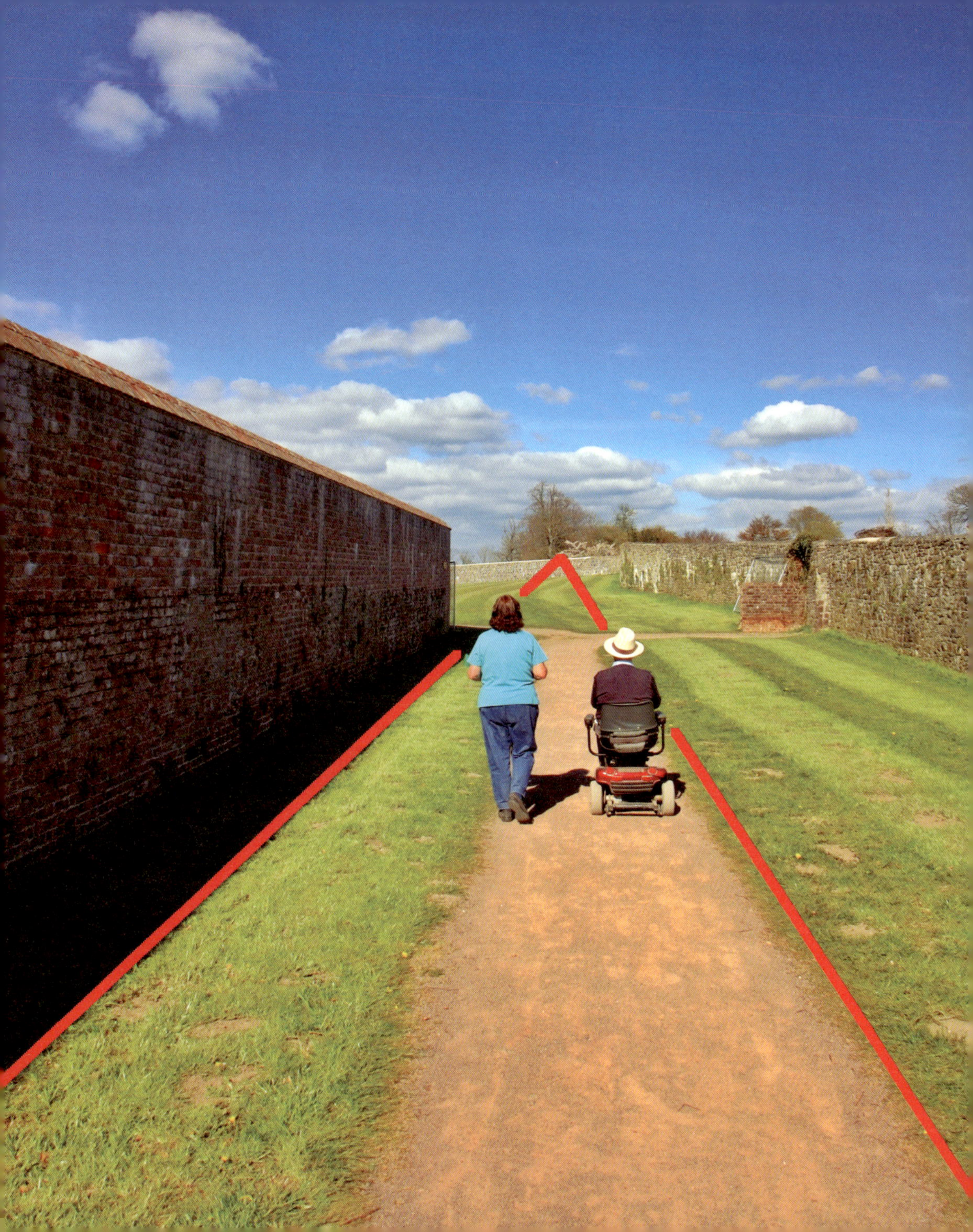

Leading lines

Lines were a punishment at school. They're a reward in photography. They can lead a viewer's eye into a picture, add depth and make it more dynamic.

Including horizontal lines in your composition tends to divide the picture into layers, giving a restful feeling. Vertical lines are more dynamic, giving a picture tension. Diagonal lines give a strong sense of movement.

And don't think that lines need to be straight ones. Look out for flowing, fluid curved lines, too. You can find them in rows of crops on a contour, ripples on water or the bends of a freeway.

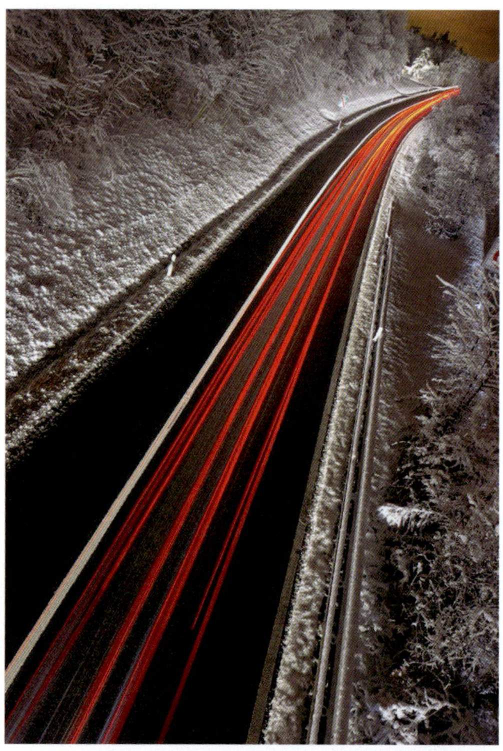

Diagonals give a powerful sense of movement.

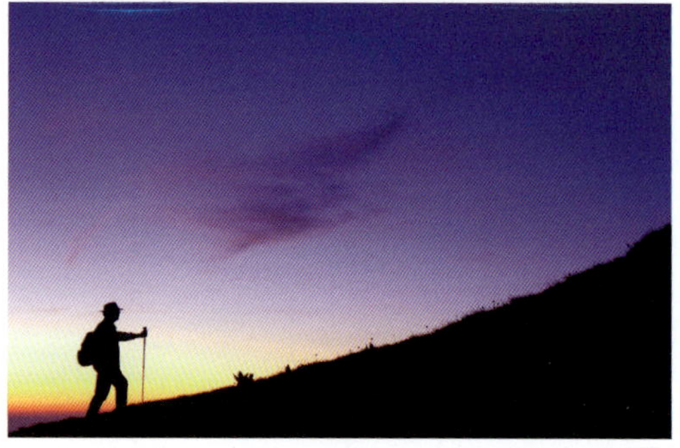

Upward curving lines can give a positive feel to an image. And the silhouette against the dawn sky simplifies this photograph.

Patterns

As has already been pointed out, one of the keys to producing great photographs is training your eye to 'see', rather than just 'look'. Discovering repeating patterns in everyday scenes is an example of this. Such patterns can be found in the most unlikely places … rows of parked cars, buildings, bookends. Look around you and you will see them in many places.

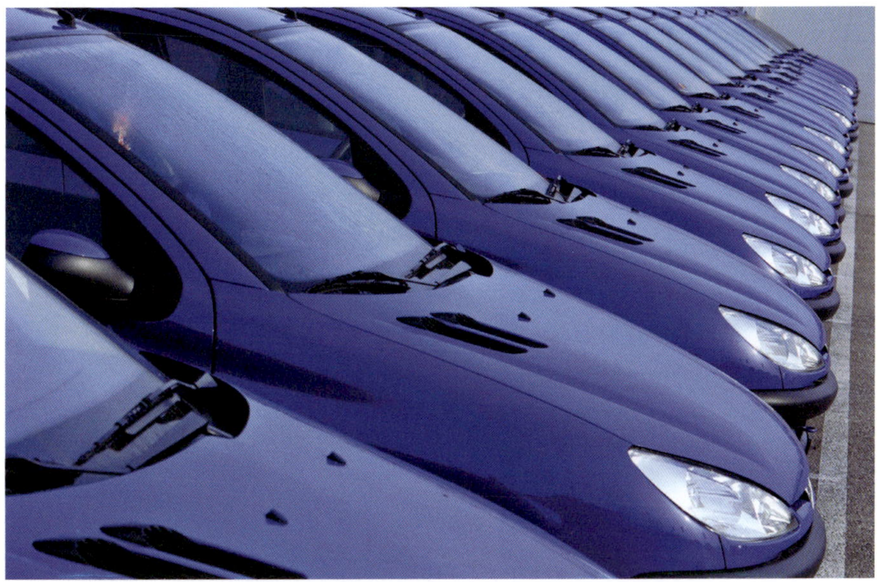

Strong graphic images can be found in everyday places. This was taken with a telephoto lens to isolate the pattern of the line of cars.

Back off!

A telephoto lens can help accentuate certain patterns by magnifying the relevant part of a scene, so cutting out extraneous 'junk'. With a telephoto you can also move further away from your subject and still get it a reasonable size in your image. Being able to move further away alters the perspective, which can also boost the impact of a pattern.

Upside down

One way of improving your compositional 'eye' is to turn your pictures upside-down. Doing this changes it into an abstract, allowing you to see how the shapes and lines relate to each other … or don't relate, as the case may be.

If your upside-down picture looks good and has balance and harmony, it will look even better the right way up.

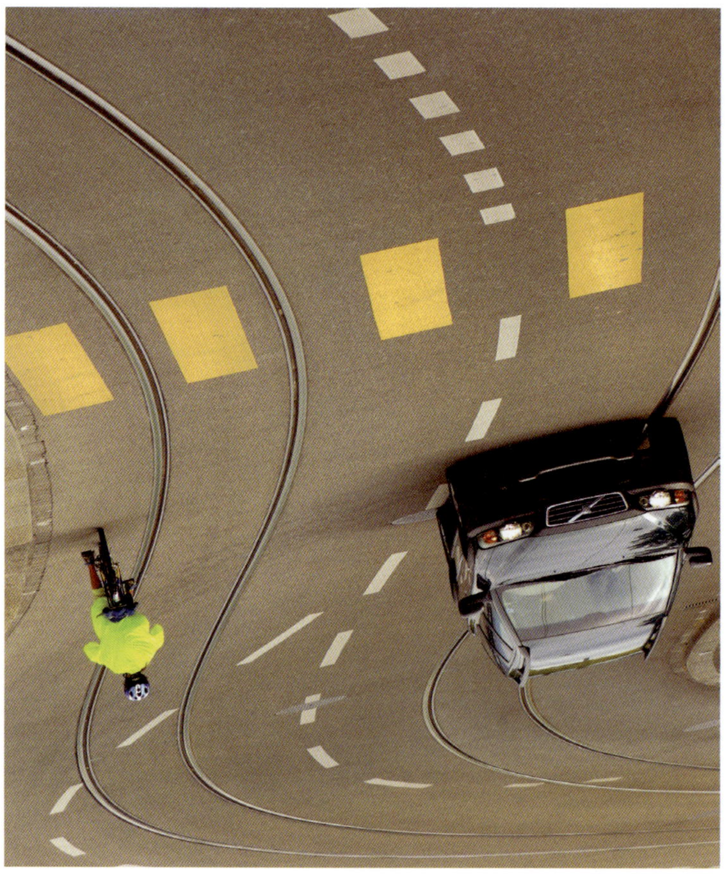

Looking at an image upside down emphasizes the compositional elements.

A moving experience

If you are photographing a scene with strong movement in it, think about what you want to portray, and compose accordingly.

For example, if you are photographing a sailboarder, zipping across a lake from right to left, his position will affect the 'interpretation' of your image. As has already been pointed out, having the sailboarder dead center gives the least interesting composition.

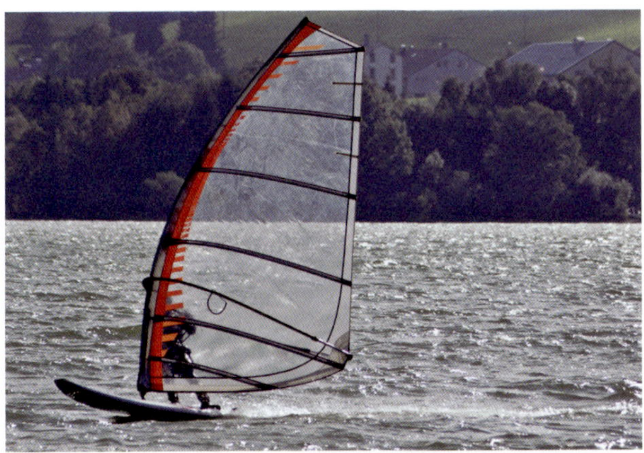

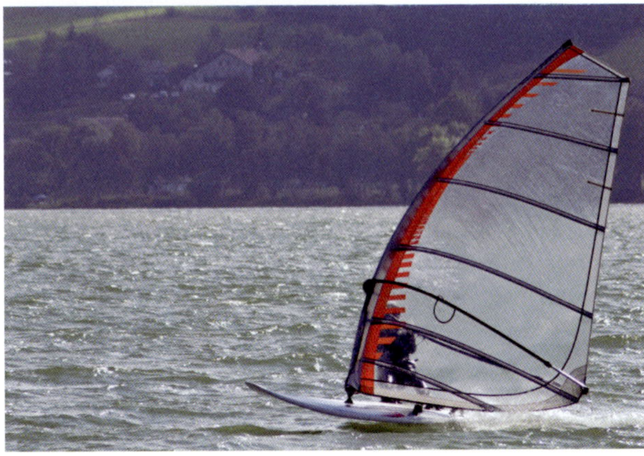

A photograph with the subject moving out of the frame gives a different feel from one with it moving into the frame (see overleaf).

If he is on the right, he is sailing in to the picture, and for most people this makes most sense. It seems 'complete', with space for the board to sail in to.

If he is on the left he is sailing out of the photograph, which raises the question, "Where's he going?" This adds tension to the composition.

The two images, though very similar, will have a different feel to them.

On the lookout

The same principle applies to static portraits, too. If your subject is sideways on and looking 'in' to the image, with more space in front of her face than behind her head, the image seems complete and raises no questions.

If, on the other hand, she is looking out of the image, with more space behind her head than in front, the question your viewer asks is, "What's she looking at?"

QUICK T!P

For most of us in the Western world, capturing a subject moving from right to left gives a slightly more 'edgy' feeling to a photograph than movement in the opposite direction. The reason? We are used to reading from left to right, so movement in that direction seems more natural.

Let's get this straight

Unless you've had a few too many beers, the horizon is usually horizontal. That's why it's called the horizon. Try to keep it that way in your photographs. Yachts look distinctly odd, sailing uphill. If you have a grid line option in your viewfinder, switch it on to help you keep things straight.

QUICK T!P

A sloping horizon can be straightened later using image editing software. But the correction means losing a portion of the image around the edges. The more the tilt, the more you lose. Get it right in camera!

You're exaggerating!

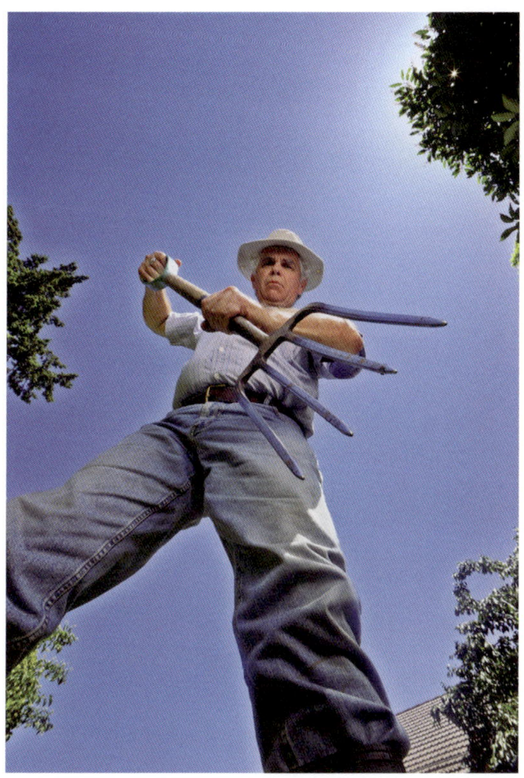

One of the most effective ways of producing memorable photographs is to exaggerate some feature. For example, get close to your subject with a wide angle lens. Or use a telephoto lens to magnify it. Try selecting an unusual angle, photographing from very low down so your subject towers above you. Or exaggeration can work in the opposite direction. Photograph from above so your subject looks ant-like. There are many ways of exaggerating. Be bold and experiment.

Gardening is an everyday occupation and could give everyday photographs. But a low viewpoint and a wide angle lens adds drama.

Have a heart

Try to include a 'heartbeat' in your pictures whenever possible: in other words, some human or animal figure. It doesn't matter how big or small the 'heartbeat' is. Its presence makes the picture more interesting immediately (see overleaf).

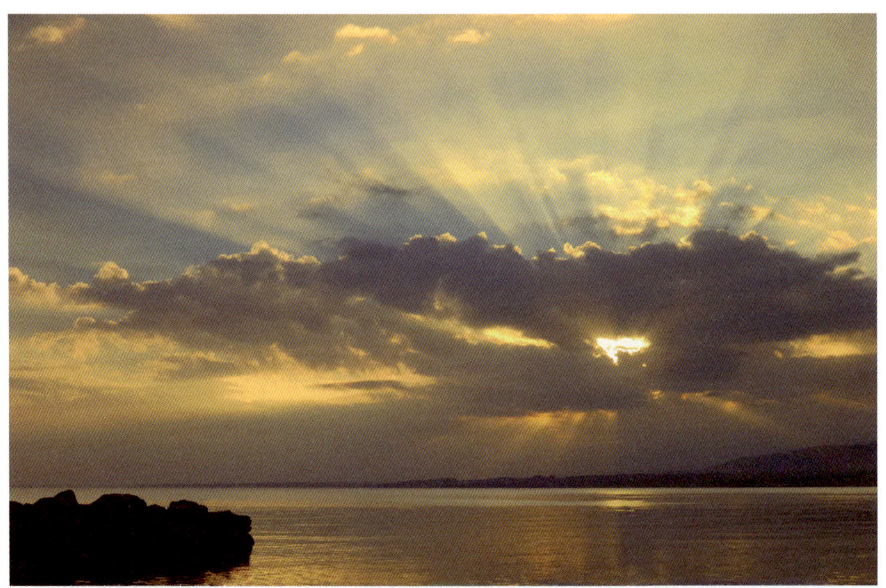

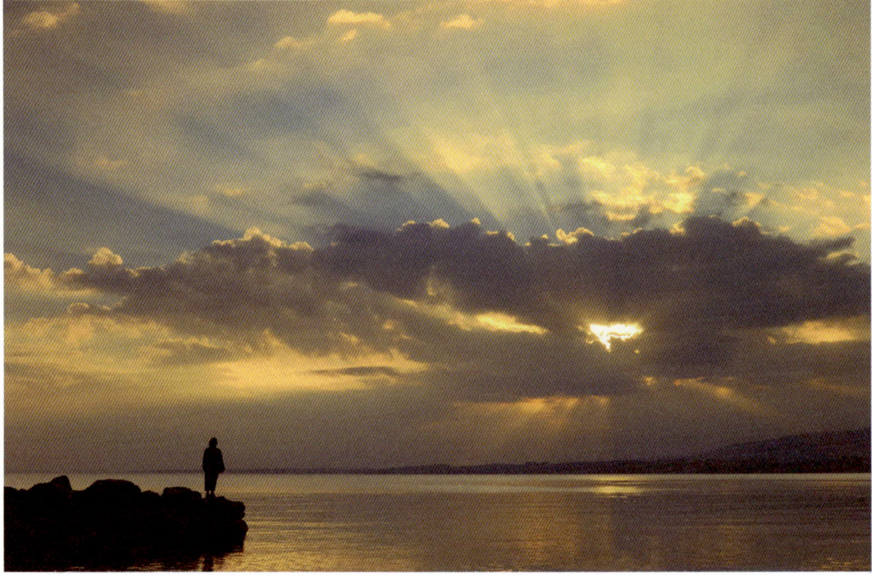

What a difference a 'heartbeat' makes!

What you see is not what you get

Be careful. What you see isn't necessarily what you'll get if you are composing through the viewfinder. The viewfinder of a compact camera is not on the same plane as the lens. Therefore, what you see may not be *exactly* what you will get in the final photograph. This is called the 'parallax error', and it means that parts of an image can be lost – usually something vital – while unwanted bits may be included at the opposite side. Experiment with your camera to familiarize yourself with how the viewfinder image differs from the photo you get. It won't be much, but it may be significant and you'll curse when, in that one-and-only opportunity to photograph the Queen of Sheba, you cut off the top of her head.

If you are composing using the screen at the back of the camera, or with SLR cameras, the parallax error doesn't apply because you are viewing the scene through the lens. However, the image sensor may still not record absolutely everything that you see. Very often there is a narrow band around the edges which does not show in the final photo. Once again, experiment to discover the way your camera handles this.

Can't get no satisfaction

Never be satisfied with your first shot. Walk around your subject (if you can). Get closer to it, or further away. Get down low or climb up high. Try lying down on the ground. Explore all your options. That is the only way to find those great compositions.

QUICK T!P

Photographing from ground level is one of the simplest ways of getting a non-distracting background. It usually isolates your subject against the sky.

Now be a lawbreaker

Now you know the rules of composition … break them. Sometimes by breaking the rules you create something special, giving you the creative edge that makes an image stand out.

For example, sometimes it pays to have your horizon sloping. The diagonal composition can give a sense of motion and speed. Another example – in a portrait you usually want your subject fully framed. But, for a change, why not have her cheekily peeping into the picture from the side?

With a digital camera you can experiment and see the results instantly. If it doesn't work you can rub it out and no one will know.

DID YOU KNOW …

'Red eye' comes from the light of a flash passing through the blood vessels that lie over the retina at the back of the eye. Some flash equipment flashes a few times before the picture is taken so that the iris of the subject's eye will close down, minimizing the effect.

We may prefer images that obey the Thirds Rule because the eyes and mouth of the human face are arranged this way.

Pinhole cameras are unique in that they don't need a lens, just a tiny hole. They require long exposures, but have a massive depth of field.

You can experiment with pinhole photography by replacing your lens with a camera body cap that has a tiny hole drilled in it. Try to get the smallest hole possible. See my blog for instructions on how to do this.

Worldwide Pinhole Photography Day is celebrated on the last Sunday in April.

Chapter summary

- Have a subject in your photograph.

- Keep it simple.

- Look at background, foreground and corners for stray objects.

- Frame your subject to focus attention on it.

- Use the rule of thirds.

- Avoid placing your subject in the center spot.

- Use shapes and lines to emphasize composition.

- Keep the horizon straight.

- Look at your photos upside down to 'see' composition.

- Include a 'heartbeat'.

- Never forget you can break the rules.

I never set out to photograph a landscape … My first thought is always of light.

Galen Rowell

The Light Fantastic

Chapter 4

The Light Fantastic

Photography is all about light. That's where the name originates. Loosely translated from Greek, 'photo' means 'light' and 'graph' means 'drawing'. When you're creating photographs the two most important factors are the quality of the light, and the amount of it. They can make the difference between your picture being a glowing masterpiece, a flat gray bore, or a gloomy rectangle.

But if the light is wrong … too dim, too harsh, or from the wrong direction … what can you do? Don't worry. You have more control than you imagine. And if you are working indoors, you have total control. This means that, with a little work, foresight and creativity, you can achieve remarkable things with light. This chapter will show you how.

Expose yourself?

In photography 'exposure' means the amount of light that you allow into the camera to create the image. This is controlled by two settings – the aperture of the lens and the shutter speed.

The aperture is the opening of the lens, like the iris of your eye, and is expressed as an 'f-number' (f5.6 … f8 … f11… and so on). Confusingly, the larger the f-number the smaller the opening. So, for example, f5.6 is a larger opening than f11 and allows more light into the camera. If you want to remember this 'Alice in Wonderland' arrangement, just think 'ALIS' (*Aperture – Large Is Small*).

The shutter speed is the length of time the shutter is open, and is expressed in fractions of seconds (1/125th … 1/250th … 1/500th and so on). This is more straightforward – the shorter the shutter speed, the less light gets into the camera.

The two settings are related, so if you double the shutter speed you must halve the aperture to let the same amount of light into your camera.

Although most cameras can set these for you automatically, it is much better if you know how to control them yourself. This will allow you to extend the range of conditions in which you can take photos, and will also allow you to become more creative.

Over and under

Over-exposure is when too much light enters the camera and the picture looks pale, and washed-out. You are either using a shutter speed that is too slow, or have the lens aperture open too wide.

And, guess what? When too little light is allowed into the camera the picture looks dark and gloomy. That's under-exposure. You are either using a shutter speed that is too high, or an aperture that is too small.

In general, if you're going to make a mistake, try to under-expose. A passable picture can often be retrieved from an under-exposed image using image-editing software. This is even more likely if you are shooting RAW files, which are more forgiving.

But in an over-exposed image the brighter parts of a picture are likely to be 'burned out'. Gone for good. They are pure white and no detail can be retrieved from those areas.

In brackets

To be sure of capturing that never-to-be-repeated shot perfectly, try 'bracketing'. This means taking three pictures in quick succession, one at the indicated exposure, one over-exposed by opening the aperture one 'click' (one 'stop' in photographic terms) and another under-exposed by the same amount. Then you will be sure to get one right.

Some cameras even have automatic bracketing. All you have to do is switch it on and press the shutter three times. The camera takes care of changing the settings.

Don't have hist-erics

Yikes! You press a button and suddenly a graph appears on the viewing screen at the back. What's that all about?

Don't switch it off in a panic. The graph is called a histogram. And, if you know how to read it, the histogram can give you valuable information about the exposure. It shows the brightness levels along the bottom axis (from darker on the left to brighter on the right) and number of pixels of each brightness level up the vertical axis.

Unless you are taking very dark subjects (e.g. silhouettes) or very light ones (e.g. snow scenes) you should aim for an evenly-formed curve (sometimes called a 'bell curve') with the graph rising from the left, to a peak somewhere in the middle, then dropping down to the right.

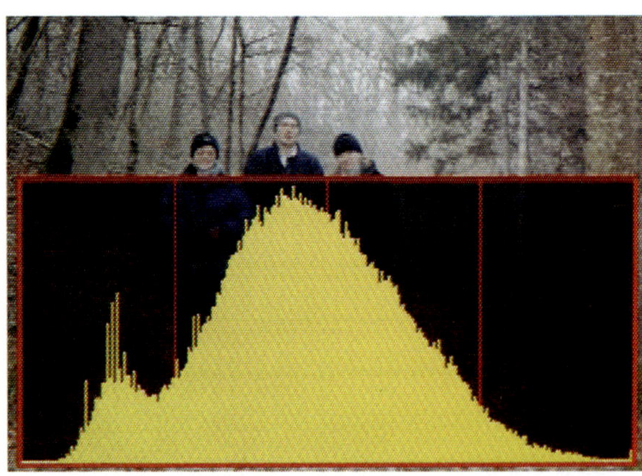

The histogram for a correctly-exposed image shows a typical 'bell curve'.

If the high point of the graph is skewed heavily to the left, your image is probably under-exposed and shadow detail will be lost. If the graph is squished up against the right side, the image is likely to be over-exposed.

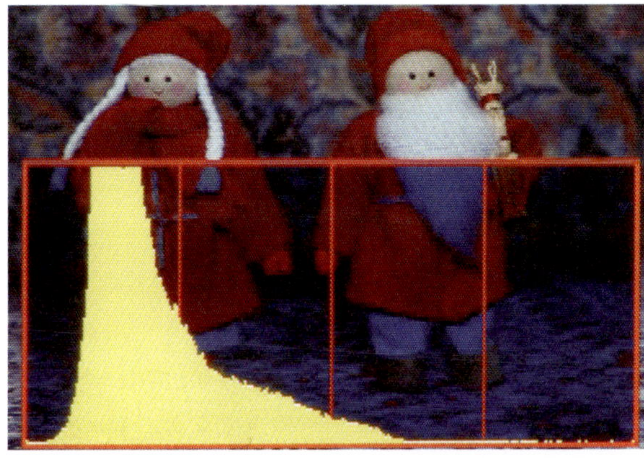

If the photograph is under-exposed the histogram will be pushed over to the left side.

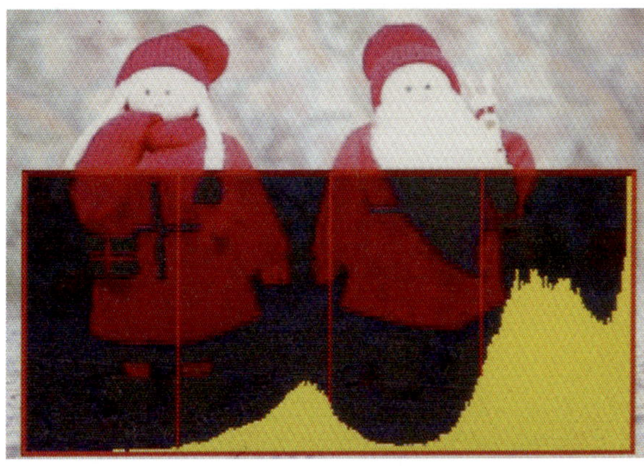

An over-exposed image will have the peak of the histogram towards the right edge.

If your camera will show a histogram, use it! It is a useful tool that can help you get your exposures correct.

Spot on

Most cameras measure the total amount of light they're 'seeing' and set the exposure automatically. This is called 'Averaging Mode' and generally works well. It means that you don't have to do a lot of calculating. But never forget that your camera is only a machine. It can be fooled easily.

For example, if you are taking a photograph of someone against a very bright background such as the sky, your camera will 'average out' all the light it is receiving. It is trying to get as much of it correctly exposed as possible and doesn't know that you're interested in the person. As the sky is a large area, and very bright, it will skew the average. In other words, the camera will get the sky blue … and your subject will come out as a dark, under-exposed blob.

In a case like that, check to see if your camera has a 'Spot Metering' mode. With Spot Metering the camera only measures the light from a very small part of the scene. This is usually indicated in the viewfinder by a red square. Switch your camera to Spot Metering, compose so that the measuring point is on your subject (or shift it around in your viewfinder), and your subject will come out correctly exposed.

QUICK T!P

When you've finished using Spot Metering, switch back to 'Averaging' straight away. If you forget, and leave it on you may get unpredictable results next time you take a photograph.

Blinking easy

Some cameras have a setting for the viewing screen where the burned-out highlights blink on and off. Use this to help you determine if you've got the exposure right. A few tiny spots winking at you – highlights on reflective surfaces for example – are okay. But if you've got large areas flashing madly then reduce the exposure a little. That is, of course, assuming you don't want large areas of pure white in your image. But, maybe you do … such as a pure white background. In that case use this facility to see if you are achieving your aim.

Wakey wakey!

The best natural light is at sunrise or sunset. At those times the sun is low in the sky, the light is softer and shadows less harsh. The sun also illuminates things in a way that brings out texture, and can produce striking shadows. Imagine, for example, the early dawn light, streaming through trees.

Of the two low-light times of day, dawn usually has the better light. The air tends to be clearer at that time so the colors will be different – wonderful pinks, purples and blues of the early-morning sky.

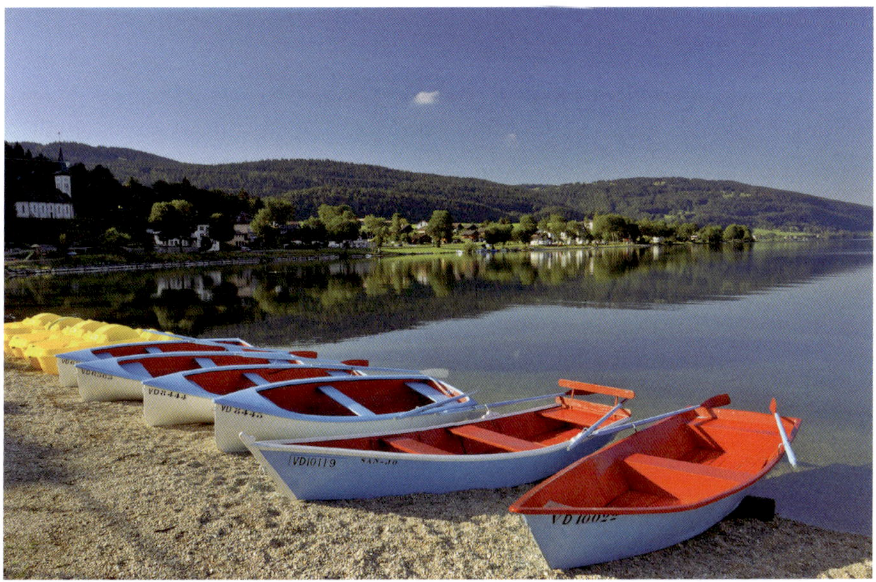

In the early morning the light is soft and low, the boats are still beached, and the water is calm. In another half-hour or so everything will have changed.

There are other benefits to dawn. Even the most touristy places will be eerily empty. And if you're interested in nature photography, many mammals are out and about at that time. On the other hand, insects are often sluggish because of the cooler temperatures, so will allow an approach for close-up photography. On top of that, the air is usually still – which is ideal for capturing easily-disturbed flowers.

Yes … it means clambering out of your lovely warm bed at 4:30am. But it's worth the effort.

Make a plan

But don't just get up early, stagger outside and wander at random. The early morning peace and light does not last long and you'll be wandering in the best of it. Plan your foray in advance, working out where the sun is going to rise, looking at the weather forecast and investigating the best spots. (For sunrise/sunset tables, check the newspaper, or see the appendix for where you can get online information.)

On-camera flash

Try not to use the dinky little flash that's built-in with most cameras. It gives flat lighting, creates harsh shadows and causes 'red-eye' in your subjects. It's true that some cameras can remove red-eye, or you can do it with an image-editing program. But you can't do anything about the light and shadows.

About the only time that flash has any value is to 'fill in' when there are strong shadows, for example, in bright sunlight (see 'This is filling', below).

What's the alternative?

If your camera has a 'hot shoe' then use a separate flash gun. External flash units are much more powerful and flexible in how they can be used. Try to get one that has a rotating head so that you can use 'bounce flash' (see 'Bouncing off the walls').

Failing that, you could carefully tape a layer or two of white cotton (your handkerchief, if it's clean) or tissue paper over the built-in flash to diffuse the light and reduce its harshness.

Watch out sunshine!

Many basic photographic guides will tell you to take pictures with the sun behind you. That's good general advice. But it's also a rule to be broken frequently.

The problem is that, with the sun directly behind you, the light is head-on for your scene, and tends to be flat. In addition, if you are taking pictures of people they will be squinting to keep the glare out of their eyes.

Instead, try photographing with the sun to one side, or even into the sun (but beware of lens flare). You could, for example, get a dramatic portrait of someone if you take the picture into the sun, using a low viewpoint so that they tower over you, blocking the sunlight.

But won't they come out as a black silhouette?

Not if you use spot metering. Or fill-in flash …

This is filling

The one time that the little on-camera flash can be useful is when you are taking photos in bright sunlight.

Flash in daylight? Why?

Because bright sunlight casts harsh shadows, and the flash will fill these in. Not surprisingly, the technique is called 'fill-in flash'.

Of course, don't bother doing this with landscapes. But if you are taking pictures of people it will help eliminate dark shadows under the nose and chin. It will also add a sparkle to their eyes. Or if you are taking pictures of flowers, it will illuminate the nooks and crannies between the petals. Professional photographers regularly use this technique. It's one of their biggest 'secrets'.

Reflect on this

Another simple but useful lighting accessory is a reflector. It can be used portraiture, or for photographing objects or flowers. You can buy reflectors from camera shops, but a piece of white card works just as well. Alternatively, stick a sheet of slightly crumpled cooking foil to a piece of cardboard. It is better to use crumpled foil because the creases help diffuse the light.

Why not make a variety of reflectors of different shapes, sizes and colors? Use yellow or orange card, or gold foil, to reflect a warm tone. Make a horseshoe-shaped one to fit around things. There are many possibilities, and a selection of reflectors will help you control light precisely.

Always be aware of where the light is coming from … and where it could come from. You may find a wonderful view one afternoon, but it is head-on into the light and impossible to photograph successfully. If you can, try returning the next morning. It may well be perfectly-lit at that time.

Running a temperature

Light is not always what it seems. To our eyes, daylight and artificial light appear to be the same. But that's because our brain compensates for the differences. If you buy a jacket without looking at it in the light of day, you could regret your choice when you step out into the street. The 'color temperature' of artificial light is warmer than that of sunlight.

Your camera can also make up for the different color temperatures through a feature called 'Auto White Balance'. This usually works pretty well, but if you want to be certain of getting the colors right it's best to set the white balance manually … to sunlight, shade, clouds, incandescent, fluorescent or flash … depending on the light source.

Getting the blues … or the oranges

Some photographers tweak the colors in their images by using filters in front of the lens. For example, orange ones make sunsets more vivid, or blue ones enhance tropical skies.

If your camera lens doesn't take filters you can achieve the same effects by changing the white balance settings. Say you're on vacation in that tropical paradise and you want to make the sky and sea a bit bluer. Switch the manual white balance to fluorescent light and see how that works. Or if you want a stronger effect, use the incandescent lamp setting.

Then, when the sun goes down over the ocean, try switching the white balance to 'cloudy' to enhance the golden colors of the sunset. Or switch to 'shade' for an even stronger effect.

QUICK T!P

If you are working with RAW files, it is better to set your camera to the correct color balance, and play with the colors when you process your photos on the computer. You will have much finer control, and will always be able to go back to the original if you make a complete hash of it.

No business like snow business

"My camera's gone haywire. It was a crisp, white winter scene, with the kids making a snowman. But the snow's come out gray!"

No, your camera isn't on the blink. It's the Automatic Metering mode again, which works on the principle that any photo you take will have a whole range of shades from dark to light. It doesn't know that most of a snow scene is brilliant white. As a result it tries to average everything out, resulting in that dirty gray.

The way around this is to be cleverer than the camera. Note the exposure reading it is giving – the aperture and the shutter speed – then change to manual and set your camera to over-expose by 1 to 2 stops. In other words, open the aperture by 1-2 clicks, or lower the shutter speed by the same amount. Do that, and your snow will be brilliant white again.

QUICK T!P

Some cameras have a snow/beach setting. But it is better to use manual exposure if you can. That can be fine-tuned far more precisely.

Fooling around

If you don't have a snow/beach setting and you don't want to use the manual option, you can often fool the camera into giving the correct exposure. Point it at an area of many colors and depress the shutter button halfway to activate the automatic exposure. Then keep it pressed to lock the exposure reading while you swing around to the snow scene.

ISO seesaw

When the light is too low you may be tempted to raise the ISO (International Standards Organization) setting on your camera. This controls the sensitivity of the chip. The higher the ISO number the more sensitive the chip is to light. ISO 100 or 200 are used for most situations and give the best results. But for low-light, ISO 400, and above, can be used.

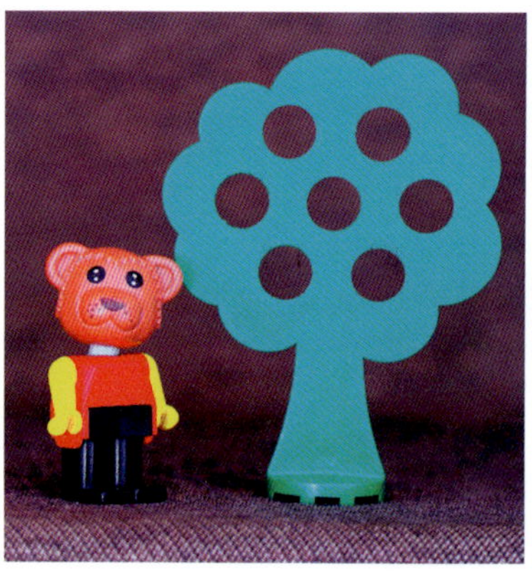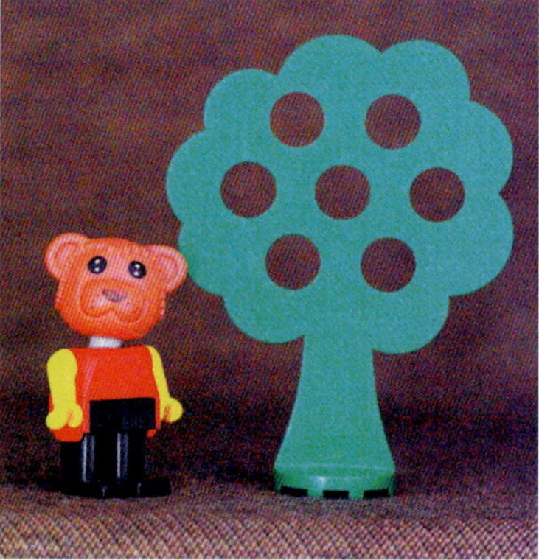

What's that noise? The first image was taken at the lowest ISO setting of the camera. A second one, of exactly the same scene under the same lighting conditions, was taken at the highest setting.

Unfortunately, there is no such thing as a free lunch. The higher the ISO setting, the more 'noisy' the picture will be. 'Noise' in digital photography is randomly-colored speckles in the image, making it look as if it's got measles. It's particularly noticeable in dark areas, such as shadows. For the best picture quality, try to keep your ISO setting as low as possible. Save the high settings for those never-to-be-repeated shots, like a lion eating Aunt Agatha at dusk.

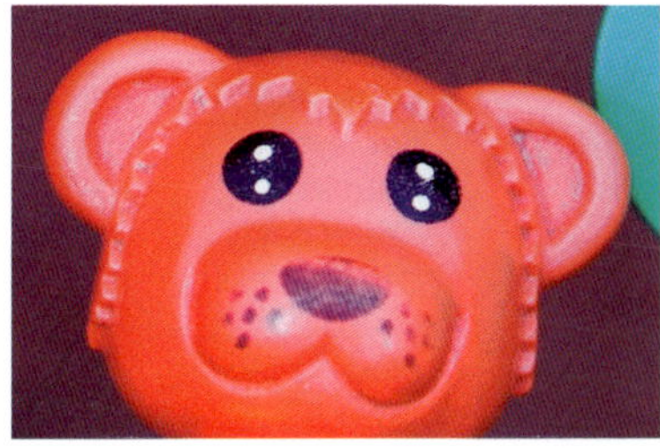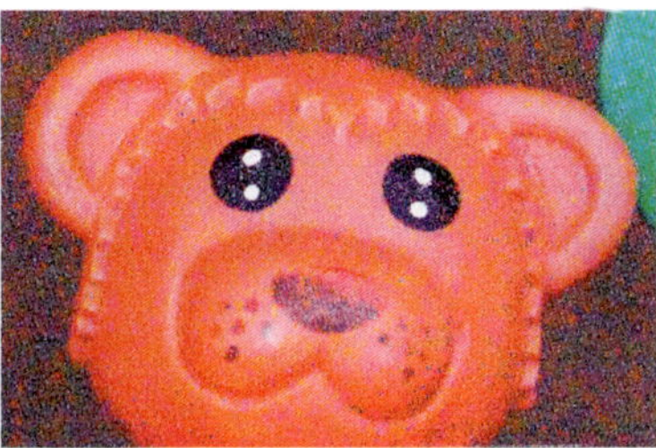

A close-up examination of the same portion of the two images clearly shows the difference.

Bouncing off the walls

Want to avoid the dreaded red-eye that makes your subjects look deranged? If you have a flash with a swivel head, turn it to point at the ceiling or a wall instead of straight at your subject. This bounces the light off a broad area and diffuses it, eliminating the problem. Better still, it also gives a much softer, shadow-free, flattering light.

Just be sure that the wall/ceiling is white. If it is pink, purple or green, your subjects will come out looking distinctly ill. Also, it must not be too far away. This technique won't work in a cathedral.

If you have an automatic flash, make sure that its sensor still points at your subject to get the correct exposure. If your flash doesn't have a sensor then you will need to increase the exposure by two or more stops to make up for the greater spread of the light. You can work out the increase by experiment – it depends on factors like the power of your flash, and the distance of the wall/ceiling.

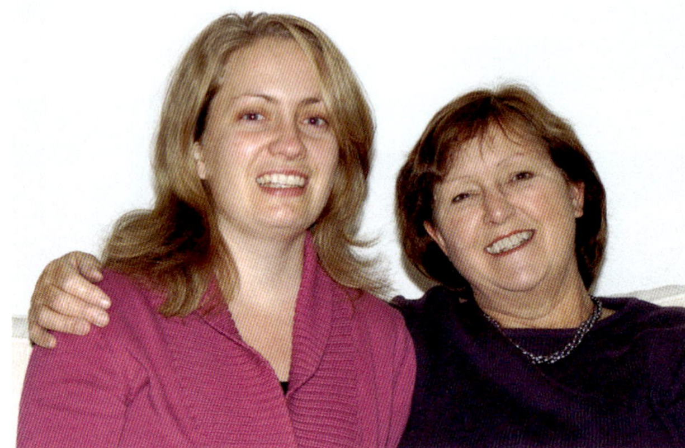

Direct flash gives harsh shadows behind your subjects, washed-out colors and flat textures. With some cameras it can also give your subjects glowing red eyes.

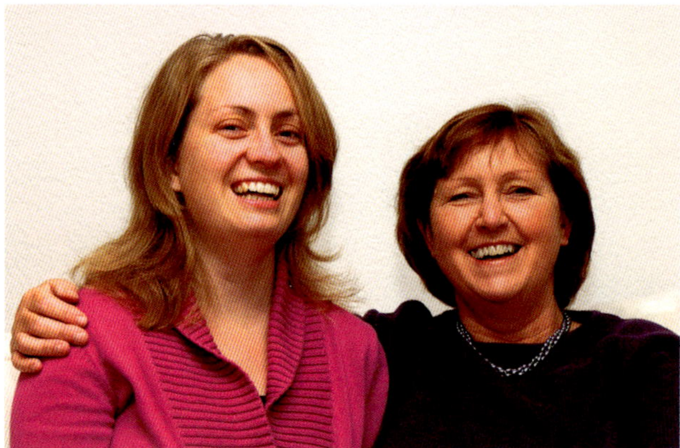

Bouncing the flash off the ceiling eliminates the shadows, gives more natural colors and brings out the texture of hair and clothes.

Showing the white card

The only problem with bounce flash is that, if you're using the ceiling, it can lead to shadows under peoples' eyes. You can eliminate this by taping a small piece of white card behind the flash head so that it sticks up to form a small reflector. This directs some of the light forwards, filling in the shadows.

Some flash guns are even equipped with a built-in card that can be pulled out when needed.

Chapter summary

- Exposure is a combination of aperture and shutter speed.

- Use the histogram to assess the correct exposure.

- Under-exposure can be more easily corrected than over-exposure.

- Early morning or late afternoon give the best natural light.

- Avoid using your on-camera flash except for filling in shadows.

- If possible bounce the light from a flash off the ceiling or a wall.

- Make some reflectors shine light into dark areas.

- Set your camera to over-expose scenes containing a lot of white, such as snow.

- Try to avoid using high ISO settings. You will get noise.

- Adjust the color temperature of an image with the White Balance setting.

" The most difficult thing for me is a portrait. You have to try and put your camera between the skin of a person and his shirt. "

Henri Cartier-Bresson

Shooting
People

Chapter 5

Shooting People

People love portraits … portraits of other people. But face the camera for one yourself? For most people that usually ranks with a visit to the dentist on a list of pleasurable activities.

So, if you are intending to do a bit of portrait photography, your first challenge will be to put your subject at ease. The best way to do this is to keep things relaxed and informal. And use the simplest of set-ups. You can achieve beautiful effects with nothing more than the light coming in through a window. In fact, you already have an excellent portrait studio in your house …

Your personal portrait studio …

… is in the bathroom.

Yes, bathrooms are ideal for portrait photography because they are usually painted white and have lots of reflective surfaces. On top of that, bathroom windows are made of frosted glass. All this gives a beautiful soft light.
Try this …

- Drape a suitable backdrop over the shower bar … you don't want the bathroom fittings in your portrait.

- Pose your subject in front of it. A comfy chair may help.

- Turn off the bathroom lights and …

- Shoot away.

- If you want to add some light then aim your flash at the white wall/ceiling to give a diffused result.

Agreed, it may be a little cramped. But the results will speak for themselves. And the hire charges are very reasonable.

The bathroom is also an ideal place for cleaning your digital camera's sensor. No, not under the cold tap! See the 'Camera care' section, chapter 10.

Beyond the bathroom

Another approach for portraiture is to choose a setting that says something about your subject. You might, for example, consider taking a portrait of a farmer leaning over a gate, a writer against a background of books, or a cook buying produce at the market.

And, if you are taking portraits outdoors, choose an overcast day. The light is softer and more flattering.

The living daylights

So, you can't afford those fabulous professional strobe units with umbrella reflectors and softboxes for your portraits.

Don't worry. Use daylight.

Despite all their equipment, many professionals prefer daylight because of its qualities. And one of the best sources of daylight is a large window, out of direct sunlight.

Sit your subject down next to it. Control the light by moving her closer or further away from the window. Sitting her closer will result in greater contrast between two sides of her face. Sitting her further away will give a more even lighting.

QUICK T!P

If one side of your subject's face is too dark, fill in the shadows with one of the reflectors you've made.

Let there be light

There are other sources of light, too …

Table and bedside lamps, with shades on, give a warm diffused radiance. Desk lamps give a harder more directional light. Both use tungsten bulbs which will give photographs a strong orange cast. Don't worry, you can correct this by altering the white balance setting to tungsten light or by using a blue filter.

Firelight and candlelight give wonderfully soft glows, but the light levels for both are very low, so will need long exposures of a second or more, and your subject will have to sit super-still. So this technique is definitely not suitable for children.

Confidence trick

When you are taking portraits, you are in control. Appear confident, as if you've done this sort of thing a thousand times before. Plan your session and have everything set up in advance. Nothing is more likely to give your model an attack of nerves if you are fiddling about with the camera and lights whilst he/she is sitting there helplessly. And if things do go wrong, keep your cool and act decisively.

White, and it's right

If you are using flash to illuminate a portrait then you should soften the light, either by bouncing it off the ceiling/walls or by using some sort of diffuser like a sheet of white cloth. Direct flash will give horribly harsh results.

But, with the light bouncing all over the place, how can you set the correct exposure? Professionals use a flash meter, which costs an arm and a leg. There's another low-cost, accurate way. All you need is a sheet of pure white card and the courage to use the histogram.

Take a preliminary 'best-guess' shot with your model holding the white card just below his/her face. Then check the histogram. You will see a sharp peak towards the right-hand side (representing the pure white of the card). If the peak is hard up against the right-hand edge you are over-exposing and should reduce the amount of light a little. If the peak is towards the middle you are under-exposing, and should increase the amount of light. Aim to get that peak just fractionally to the left of the right-hand edge, and you'll be spot-on.

And how do you reduce/increase the amount of light? To reduce the amount of light, move the light sources further away, increase the shutter speed or close down the aperture. Do the opposite, in each case, to increase the amount. Simple.

Getting the wind up

If you are taking a portrait of someone with long hair (and if she doesn't mind), have a fan blowing a soft current of air on to her face from an angle. Not only will this help her keep cool, it will also move her hair slightly, giving a more 'active' feel to a portrait. Just don't have the fan too close or you'll have hair all over the place.

You must be joking

Most people feel self-conscious in front of a camera. They pose like a tailor's dummy and grin like someone is driving a nail through their foot.

So do everything you can to put your subject at ease. A cup of tea? A beer? A few jokes or a little banter? Be reassuring. Maybe put on some of their favorite music. And a little bit of flattery can work wonders too. What's more, don't forget to smile yourself. Enthusiasm is infectious.

Does my bum look big in this?

It will if you use a wide-angle setting to photograph someone's backside.

All right … so you mostly photograph people from the front. But the same principle applies. Wide angle lenses allow you to get more into a picture. However, in order to get a reasonably-sized image, you have to get close with a wide angle lens. And this distorts perspective.

If you take a portrait of your girlfriend using a wide-angle setting, her nose is going to look excessively large in relation to the rest of her face.

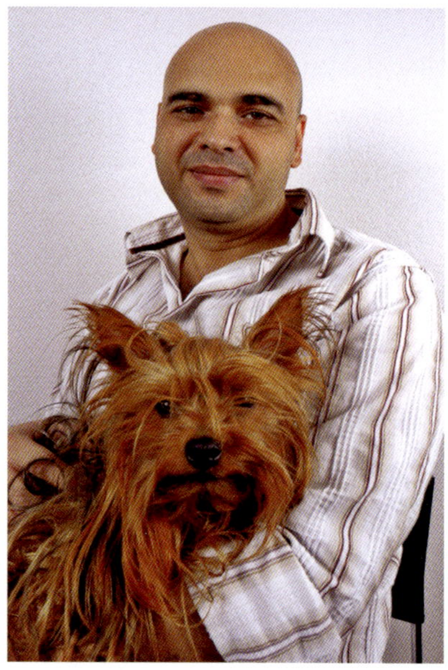

Your subject won't thank you for using a wide-angle lens.

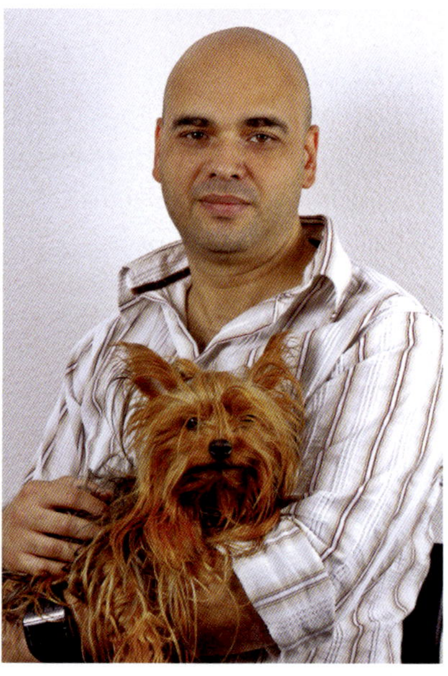

The same portrait using a 100mm lens. Proportions are much better.

In order to get the same-sized image with a telephoto lens you have to stand further away. This flattens perspective, is more flattering for portraiture, and doesn't stress relationships.

A telephoto setting of 100mm is an excellent compromise. It gives a good result without you having to be so far away from your subject that they can't hear when you tell them to say 'cheese'. No … forget the 'cheese'. There are alternatives …

Cheese is cheesy

It's well-known – saying 'cheese' shapes the mouth into a smile. But it's a wooden, boring and false one.

If you want to bring some life into your portraits, make your subjects laugh by telling them a joke. It doesn't have to be a good one. Any gag will lighten the atmosphere. Other options are to surprise them, encourage them to show emotion, or get them to tell you a story. This will animate their faces and lead to much more interesting … even revealing … photographs.

Jump to it!

Better than getting your subject to smile, ask him/her to do something unusual.

The great portrait photographer Phillipe Halsman used a technique he called 'jumpology'. He encouraged his subjects, no matter how rich, famous or powerful they were, to jump in the air. The way they jumped – exuberantly, demurely, prudishly – was wonderfully revealing of character. To see how successful this can be, just look at his pictures of Marilyn Monroe, the Duke and Duchess of Windsor or Richard Nixon.

Try that with your subjects. The idea is not copyrighted. Or get them to do something different … pull a face, pose with a favorite prop, look at the camera upside down. You will probably get some intriguing results.

Angling for compliments

Having your models pose square-on to the camera can make them look wide and confrontational. People would generally prefer to look more sympathetic. And very few people want to look wider than they are. Most would prefer to lose a few pounds.

The best way to avoid this problem is to pose your subject at a slight angle, with one shoulder a little closer to the camera than the other. But don't overdo it. Sideways on can highlight a beer belly! Turning your subject just a few degrees to one side will do the trick.

Of course, bear in mind that some subjects, such as teenaged boys, may want to look wide and confrontational …

Seriously weird

Okay, so it's best to use a medium telephoto for conventional portraits. But this is another rule to be broken. Sometimes you may want some weirdness.

For example, let's say that you are taking a portrait of little Freda, dressed up as a Halloween witch, with a warty nose. If you get up close, with a maximum wide angle setting to your lens, your witch will look seriously grotesque. Taking portraits close up with a wide-angle lens, can dramatically accentuate features. Try it with the dog, too, or with cows leaning over a fence. Experiment.

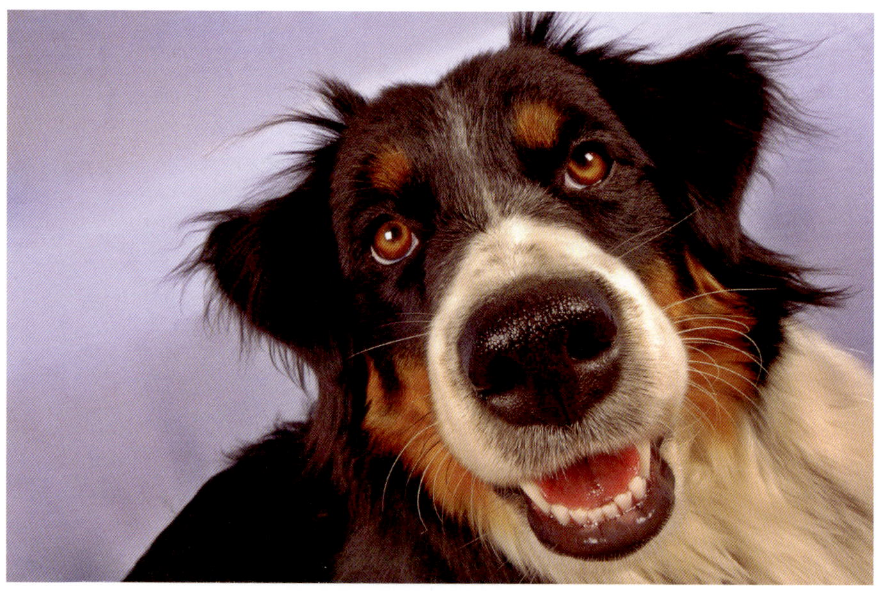

Sometimes you may want to exaggerate facial features by using a wide angle lens, close-up.

The soft touch

Sometimes a little bit of softening or blur will improve a portrait. That's right! This may sound odd, especially if you have spent a large sum of money on buying a razor-sharp lens, but it doesn't mean the image is out of focus or degraded.

Instead, it is diffused slightly, especially around the edges, using a soft focus filter. This can give a gentle, flattering feel, and help to conceal skin blemishes (yes, let's be honest, everyone has them). These filters also work well with backlighting, creating attractive haloes and enhancing the mood in scenic shots.

Smooth it yourself

If you don't want to go to the expense of buying a soft focus filter, or you want to experiment, there are two ways of achieving a similar effect in camera.

One technique is to apply a thin coating of petroleum jelly or nail varnish around the edges of an old UV or skylight filter, leaving the center clear. The advantage of this is you can vary the amount of softening according to the thickness of the smear.

Another, less messy approach is to use a piece of transparent (sheer) stocking or pantyhose. Cut off a section that is big enough to cover the camera lens with room to spare at the sides. Stretch the piece taut over the camera lens and secure it with an elastic band around the lens barrel.

You can also achieve similar effects using image editing programs, and the advantage of this is that your original, sharp image can remain untouched. However, details of how to do this are beyond the scope of this book. Websites listed in the appendix will have details.

Eye, eye captain

In a portrait, the eyes are the most important feature. Get them pin-sharp. And arrange the lighting so that there is a catch-light reflected in each one. That little sparkle adds so much life.

Try focusing on your subject's eyes whilst using a wide aperture to give a shallow depth of field. A pair of sharp eyes looking out from a hazy face can create a powerful effect.

Spectacular

Be careful if your sitter is wearing spectacles. Reflections from them can be a nightmare in portraiture, obscuring your subject's eyes with ugly flares. There are three ways of getting around this:

1. Use a pair of empty frames. This works best if you can find some frames that are the same, or very similar to the ones your subject normally wears. Does he/she have an old pair from which the lenses can be removed?

2. Angle the light source (or the subject's head if that is easier) to avoid the reflections.

3. Take the spectacles off completely and put them aside.

Don't look now

Don't think that your sitters have to look directly at the camera in a portrait session. You can also pose them informally, gazing into the distance, reading a book, or busy at work. This technique works particularly well

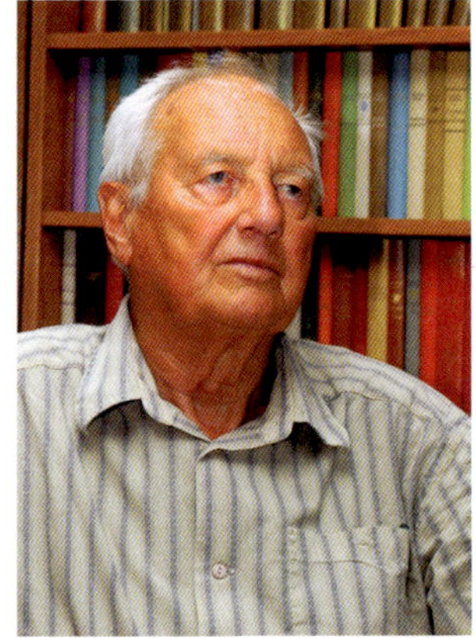

Subjects don't have to look at the camera. Gazing out of the frame adds an air of mystery.

with environmental portraiture – portraits taken in a location, such as home or workplace, associated with the subject – or if you are taking a portrait of two people. For example, with a newly-engaged couple, why not photograph them looking at each other, or interacting in another, natural way. The same technique works well for mother and child.

Hands down

One of the commonest problems that nervous subjects have is knowing what to do with their hands. They sometimes clasp them in front, which makes their fingers look like sausages. Or they rest their chin in both cupped hands, making it look as if their head is too heavy.

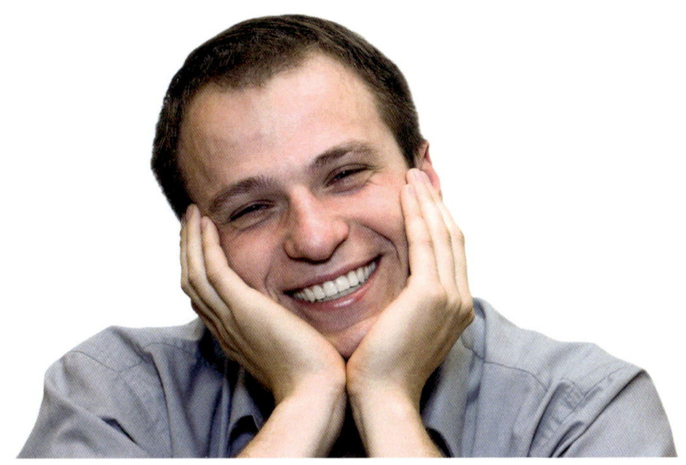

What not to do with your hands! He looks as if he's holding his face on.

In a head and shoulders shot, persuade your subject to keep her hands down. Or, if she really wants hands in a picture, have one hand raised gracefully with her chin resting lightly on the backs of her fingers in a thoughtful manner – 'lightly' being the operative word.

Alternatively, be bold. Make hands a feature. Get your little Halloween witch to form claws, or a sportsman to give the thumbs up. Think creatively.

Mug shot

The rule of thirds applies for portraits too.

When taking a picture of someone the temptation is to put their face dead center in the image. This often gives too much empty space above them and makes it look like a 'mug shot'. Try re-framing so that your subject's head is in the top third. This will include more of their body, and that's got to be more interesting than empty space.

Cut off in their prime

If you're taking portraits that show more of your subject's body, be sure not to cut them off at the joints, particularly elbows or knees. Include a bit more (or less) of the arm/leg for a more natural-looking result.

Selfish?

Artists have been producing self-portraits for centuries. Why not try the same? You can do it using the self-timer, or with the help of a mirror. If you use a mirror, the camera will show, but isn't that who you are – a photographer? Another way to do it is to use the remote release cord, which gives you more control.

At the most basic level, taking self-portraits gives you experience in lighting, camera angles and settings without the need for a model. You can experiment to your heart's content without someone getting twitchy.

Chapter summary

- There's no need for complicated equipment in portraiture. Keep it simple.

- Natural light is best. It gives flattering results, and the bathroom is an excellent place to find it.

- Experiment with other sources of light too – firelight, candlelight, table lamps.

- If you are taking formal portraits, ensure everything is ready before your sitter arrives.

- Put your subjects at ease with jokes or pleasant conversation.

- For unusual portraits make your subjects do something different.

- Avoid face-on shots. They make your subject look stocky and aggressive.

- Use a medium telephoto lens for undistorted results.

- Focus on your subject's eyes.

- People do not have to look at the camera for a portrait.

- Try self-portraits.

> *A good photograph is knowing where to stand.*

Ansel Adams

The Call
of the Wild

The Call of the Wild

A magnificent mountain range spreads out in all its glory before you. Your shutter finger works overtime until the memory card is full. But when you're back at home and you call the photos up on your computer screen your heart sinks. Where has all the glory gone?

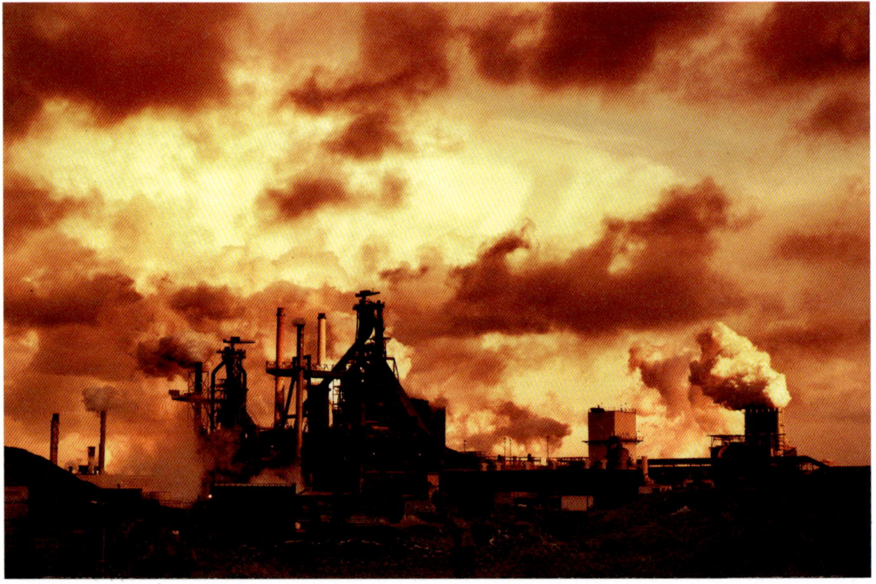

The light makes all the difference to this industrial scene.

Unfortunately, there's no getting away from a hard fact – although landscape photography is hugely popular, getting worthwhile results is difficult. The single most important factor is the quality of the light. It doesn't have to be light from a golden sun, peeping over the horizon. Dramatic landscapes are achievable when the sun is hidden. You don't even have to be in amazing scenery. Under the right lighting conditions even an old gas-works can look good.

So, success is all about being in the right spot at the right time. And that rarely happens by accident. You have to work at it and wait … and wait … and wait … until the light is right.

But, if you don't have the time to wait, there are still a number of techniques you can apply which will improve your landscapes dramatically.

Red sky at night, photographers' delight

If you want the best light, get into the habit of watching the weather forecast. If the forecaster is predicting a clear night followed by a sunny day, get up early!

But this isn't necessarily enough. To get the light just right you need to know where and when the sun is going to rise. The internet is a great source of information for this, and for many other 'ephemeris' (as they're called) – moonrise and moonset, moon phases, what planets can be seen, when satellites pass over, and more – for any place in the world.

Some of the facilities are websites, others are freeware programs that you can download and install on your computer for use even when you don't have an internet connection. Some internet sites will generate tables for your location, that you can print and carry with you. Others will show you the information graphically, on a map. Details of a selection of these are given in the appendix.

Whatever the weather

What about gales, torrents of rain, blizzards? Surely that sort of weather is too bad for photography. Isn't it best to stay indoors, curled up with a good book, or processing all those photos you took in the fine weather?

No! If you want to get some dramatic landscapes, put on your rain gear and get outside into the thick of it. You may have to wait patiently for just the right break in the clouds, but it'll be worth it. Even fog can provide some moody and mysterious landscapes.

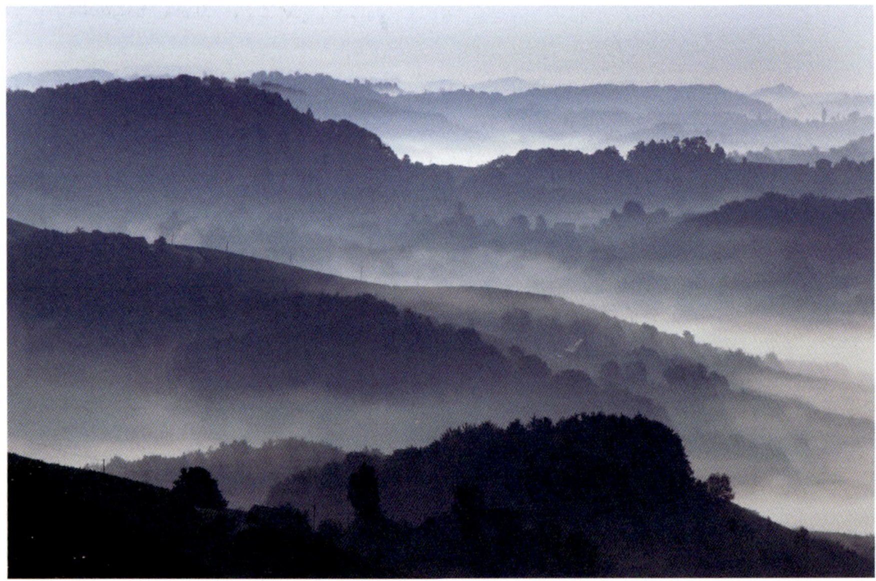

Don't put your camera away when the weather is bad.

About the only 'stay-indoors-weather' is dull, low, continuous stratus cloud with a steady drizzle falling. Time to process all your other images then.

The early bird …

… captures the best images. If you're photographing landscapes, mid-day is usually the worst time to work.

You will get far better results in the early morning or late afternoon, when the sun is lower and casts interesting shadows that bring out textures of the terrain. The light may be softer. Or, with a blazing sunrise, it may be more dramatic. In any event it will be different.

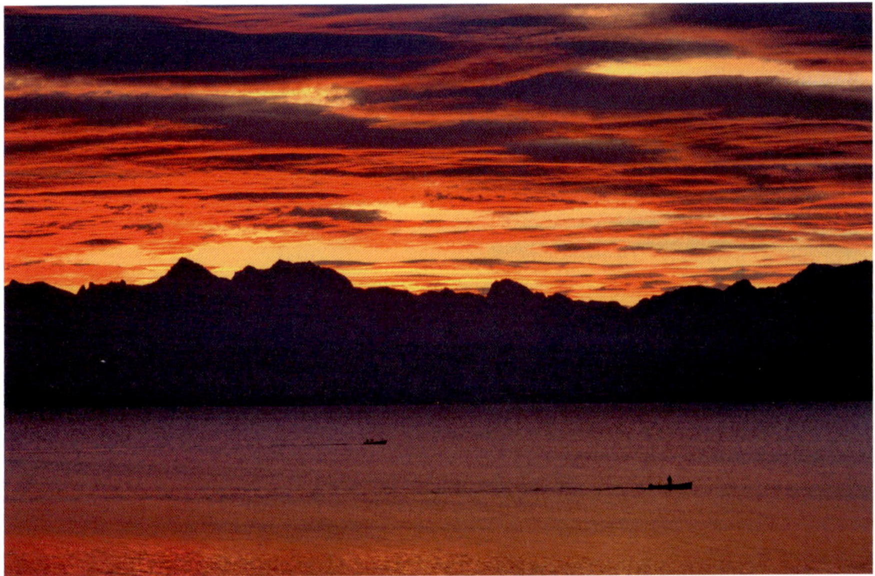

You have to be ready to capture the moment. The colors of this stunning sunrise lasted less than five minutes.

Be prepared

Unfortunately the period when the light is just right may be brief, sometimes only a matter of minutes. If you are serious about getting a good landscape picture you need to be in place, ready to start shooting, well in advance. Then you have to wait … and wait for the light. Patience is a virtue for landscape photographers.

Being subjective

One of the first temptations you have to overcome when looking at a magnificent landscape is to try to capture everything.

This almost never works. The result is disappointing because it is impossible to cram what you see with your eyes – a 100 degree view – on to that small sensor in your camera.

Instead, find a subject. It may be a dead tree, a mountain peak or, best of all, a 'heartbeat' – a living figure in the scene – that will provide a point of 'focus' for your viewer. It can also give a sense of scale to the image. A tiny figure in a vast landscape can speak eloquently as to how huge it really is.

Just remember, when you've chosen a subject, dead center is not a very interesting position for it.

Getting familiar

If you're starting out with landscape photography, first choose a familiar place. You know the scene well, you know different viewpoints and are able to assess its potential at different times in the year, different times of day and under different weather conditions. Even so, it could take several visits to get that stunning shot you're looking for.

What's in front?

When taking pictures of landscapes the tendency is to look into the distance. But consider what's nearer to you, too. The inclusion of something in the foreground draws the eye into the picture and gives a sense of depth and scale that makes a picture look three-dimensional. It could be a path, pebbles on a beach, a mossy log, wild flowers or grasses, reflections on water, anything that is natural but neutral, and not too intrinsically interesting in itself.

Depth of field again

But how do you get both foreground and background in focus at the same time? Stop right down to your smallest aperture, so you are using your full depth of field, and set your lens at its hyperfocal distance. What you see in the viewfinder may look blurred, but don't worry. When you take the picture … voila! … the iris will close and everything from about a meter away to infinity will be in focus.

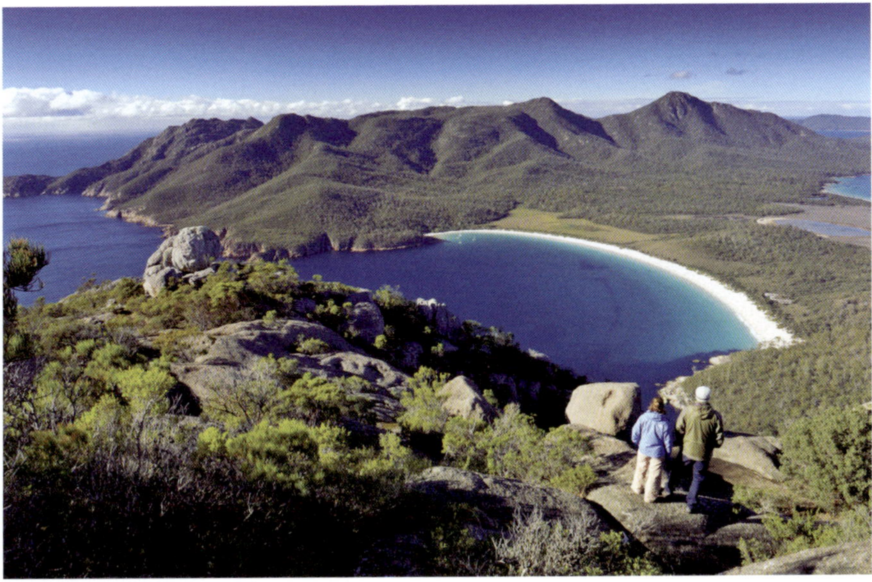

The two small figures and the section of mountainside in the foreground draw the viewer's eye into this picture.

With these settings your shutter speed will probably be slow and a tripod, coupled with a remote release (or the camera's self-timer) will be essential to avoid vibrations.

QUICK T!P

If you're using a remote release, tie a bright ribbon to it. That will reduce the chances of leaving it behind on a mountainside somewhere.

Keep a weather eye

When you are photographing landscapes, try to anticipate the short-term weather. For example, if the sky is filled with clouds, note which way they are moving. A gap in them, some distance away, may be moving towards you, bringing with it a very photogenic shaft of sunlight. Watch, and wait for it to happen.

Mist opportunity

A mist-covered view may not seem to provide many opportunities for photography. The countryside and sky will be hidden, the light dim, and everything a featureless gray. But wait … once more. The secret of success is timing. The fog will begin to lift, sooner or later. And when it does, color will return to the landscape.

The key to getting a successful shot is to take photographs at the moment when there is a balance between moody mist and the vibrant landscape. Too much mist and the scene will be that monotonous gray. Not enough and you will fail to capture the mysterious atmosphere. But be aware, the moment when mist and landscape are in perfect balance can be very short – no more than a minute or two – less if a breeze gets up. So you need to be ready.

Mist when? Mist where?

If you are keen on photographing those atmospheric misty landscapes then dawn, especially on a wind-free morning, is the best time. And the best places are low-lying land, or river valleys, where mist tends to settle. The very best spot of all is an elevated position overlooking that valley, hollow or other low-lying land.

QUICK T!P

Have a lens cloth ready while you are waiting for the mist to lift, and keep checking your lens. The humid conditions mean that droplets of water are likely to condense on the glass, ruining the contrast. If droplets do begin to form, wipe them off with the cloth.

Sky-high

Look above you. If there are dramatic cloud formations, point your camera upwards to make the sky the dominant feature. Leave the land as a mere narrow strip along the base. These 'skyscapes' can create very successful photographs, especially if you use an ultra wide-angle lens. Just remember to include a little bit of land in the image, preferably with something like trees or buildings on it. They give a sense of scale. A photograph of nothing but sky doesn't convey its 'vastness' in the same way.

QUICK T!P

Spend time sky-watching, even when you don't have your camera with you. Become familiar with the different types of cloud, how they form and move. Watch the moon as it rises, or the stars as they rotate. Just as a farmer is never wasting his time leaning on a gate watching his animals, so a photographer is never wasting time watching the sky.

Blue sky thinking

How do professional photographers get such amazingly blue skies on postcards or travel brochures?

By using a polarizing filter. This filter makes the sky bluer, giving one of the few visual effects that cannot be added later by using an image editing program.

Fit the polarizer, point the camera at the sky at right-angles to the sun's position and turn the outer ring of the filter. You will see changes immediately. Don't overdo it. If you're not careful a polarizing filter can make the sky look almost black. Note that polarization is most effective at 90 degrees to the sun. If you are taking pictures with the sun behind you, the effect is much less.

Polarizing filters also have the advantage of reducing the effect of reflections off water and leaves. This makes water look clearer, and enriches the colors of foliage.

The only disadvantage with polarizing filters is that they reduce the amount of light passing through the lens. This means a wider aperture or slower shutter speed, which can lead to camera shake.

QUICK T!P

Polarizing filters aren't cheap. When using one make sure you rotate the outer ring as if you were screwing the whole filter into the lens (i.e. anticlockwise). If you turn it the other way you could be unscrewing the filter. It falls off and … smash! … or splash!

Going round in circles

If you have a digital camera, buy a circular polarizing filter. And 'circular' doesn't refer to its shape. Most filters are the same shape – round, to fit on the front of the lens. 'Circular' refers to the type of filter.

The other type is called 'linear'. A linear polarizing filter may be cheaper but, for technical reasons, a digital camera's autofocus and exposure may not work properly with it on the front of the lens.

How can you tell the difference? The one you want should be marked 'Circular Polarizer' (sometimes abbreviated Cir, PL Cir, or CPL). If in doubt, look at a reflection through the filter whilst rotating it. When you look from the camera side of the filter the reflection should appear and disappear as you rotate it. When you look at it the other way around (as if you're looking into the camera) there will be no change. Another check is to hold the filter up against a mirror. A linear polarizer will appear gray whichever way you hold it. A circular one will appear gray one way but black when turned over.

Wide angle tangle

If you are using a polarizing filter with an ultra wide-angle lens you may find that the sky comes out in different shades of blue across your picture. This is because the polarization effect is greatest at right angles to the sun and least in line with the sun. An ultra-wide angle lens can take in a good part of this range, so making a strange darker area in the sky.

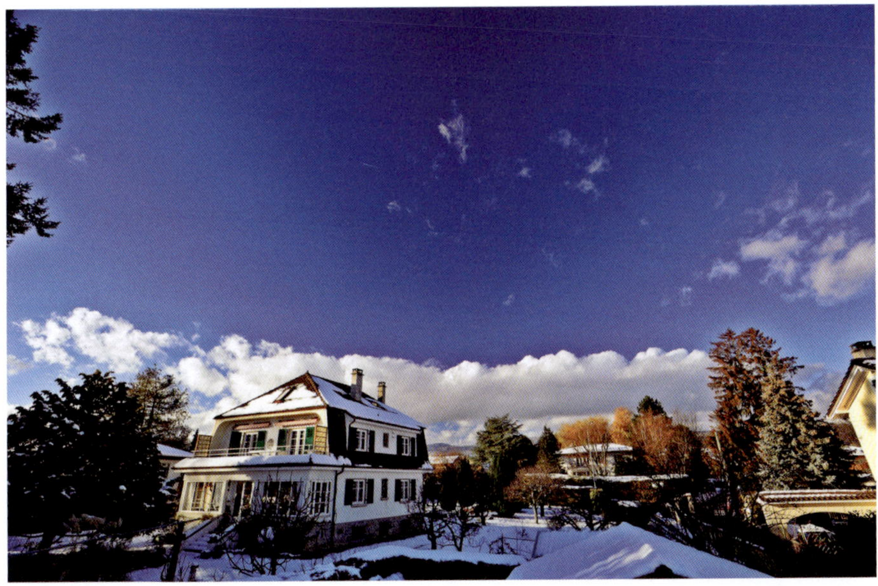

Using a polarizing filter with a wide-angle lens (17mm) has resulted in a strange darker band across the sky.

One way around this is to rotate the filter so the polarization effect is reduced and the darker patch is less noticeable. Another way is to frame your picture so that the darker patch is in a corner. It doesn't look so strange then.

Pano-rambo

To capture the drama of a broad vista try making a panorama. This can be done, at a pinch, by hand-holding the camera. But it is better to use a tripod. Ensure the head of the tripod is horizontal in all directions by using a spirit level so that when you swivel it, your panorama will not start going downhill.

Set the exposure manually so that it does not change between images, and don't use a polarizing filter. It will make the sky shade from light to dark and back again. Set your lens to its standard focal length (usually 50mm) and take a series of photographs from side to side, ensuring that each one overlaps its neighbor by about a quarter.

Then, when you get home, use a computer program to stitch the images together into a broad landscape. Details of a good freeware program are given in the appendix. You may find that there are small differences in angles and sizes of things at the joins (these will probably be worse if you have hand-held). But you can get rid of them by careful cloning and brushing in your image editing program.

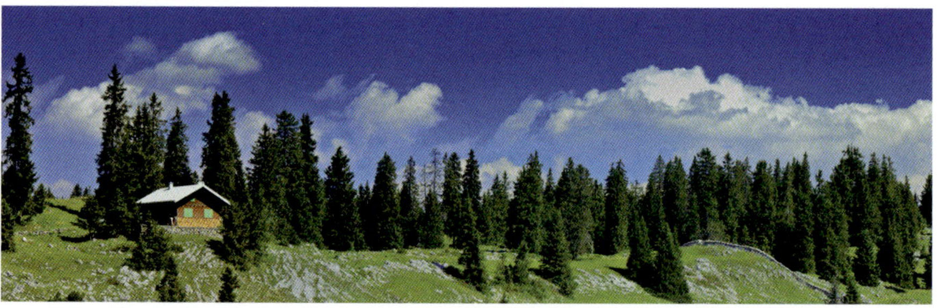

Panoramas don't have to be of distant mountains. This one is made of three images, stitched together.

QUICK T!P

Don't be tempted to use a wide-angle lens for a panorama. These lenses tend to distort images at the edges, making joining the images more difficult. Stick with a 30–50mm focal length.

Getting a head start

If you are interested in producing panoramas on a regular basis then buy, or make, a special panoramic head for your tripod.

This rotates the camera about the 'nodal point' of the lens, which is not the same as the center of the camera body. By using the nodal point you will eliminate parallax errors at the joins. Unfortunately panoramic heads are large, heavy and very expensive, so they're only suitable if you want to specialize.

However, instructions for making one at home can be found on the internet. Search on a phrase like "panoramic tripod head".

Go with the flow

Flowing water can be tricky to photograph. If you use a high shutter speed the water will be frozen in motion. Some people like this, but it does not give the sense of fluidity that is characteristic of water. Sometimes a better method is to close the aperture of your lens right down to its minimum

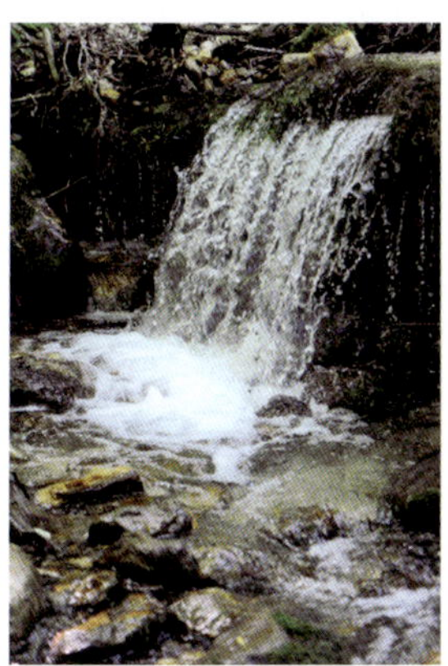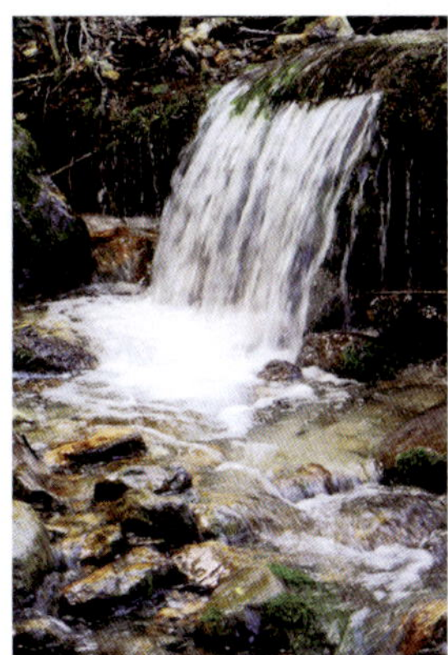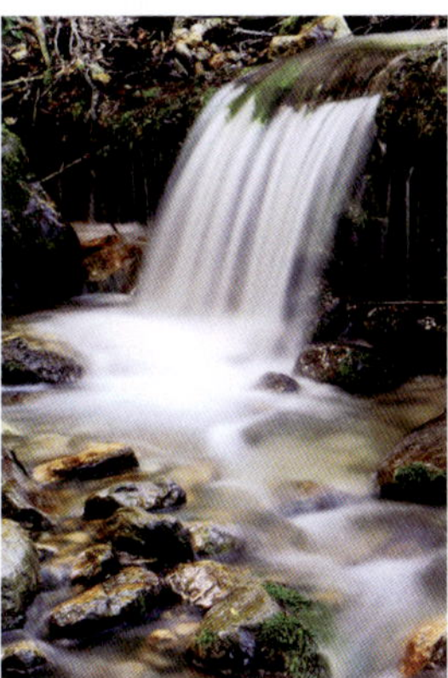

Three photographs of the same waterfall. The first used a shutter speed of 1/50th second, in the second the shutter was set to 1/10th second, and in the third the shutter speed was 2.5 seconds. Which one works best?

level (something like $f22$) so that you can use a slow shutter speed. This blurs the moving water making it look silky which gives a sense of motion.

Different shutter speeds will give different degrees of blurring. A moderately slow speed, such as 1/10 second, will give a little blur. A longer one of 2 seconds, for example, will turn the water into white diffuse streaks. Even longer ones will enhance the effect. Experiment to discover which speed gives the image you want. Note that a tripod, or some other rock-steady means of support, will be essential. You cannot hope to hand-hold the camera still enough for exposures of this length.

If you've closed down the aperture to its minimum, and reduced the ISO rating to rock-bottom and still can't get slow enough shutter speeds, then use your polarizer, or a neutral density filter (i.e. a filter which darkens but does not change color) to cut out more of the light.

Graduation day

Sunrises and sunsets are popular subjects, but tough challenges. The huge difference between the light in the sky and the darkening land means that if you set your camera to expose the sky correctly the land will turn out black. But if you set the exposure for the land, the sky will be a horrible over-exposed white.

Don't despair. A graduated neutral density filter (ND Grad) will help you overcome this problem. This is a half and half filter which shades from a neutral gray in one half to completely clear in the other and slots in front of the lens in a special holder. ND Grads come in various strengths, suitable for different lighting conditions. Position the filter in front of your lens with the neutral density part covering the sky and it will help even out the exposure. Most filter holders will let you use two filters at once so you can increase the strength to cope with extreme differences.

But, once again, be careful not to overdo it. A sky that is too dark looks unnatural.

At the double!

Another way around the problem of bright sky and dark land is to take two separate photographs, one exposed for the sky and the other for the landscape. You will have to use a tripod and be careful not to move the camera in between shots so that, apart from the different exposures, the two images are precisely the same.

Then, when you get home you can use a photo-editing software program to blend the two images. The process is called High Dynamic Range Imaging (HDRI or HDR). If you feel expert you can do it yourself, or there are specific programs or plug-ins that will do it for you.

Moonlighting

For a very different view of a landscape, try photographing it by moonlight. You'll need to choose a night when the moon is full (or close to it) and the sky is clear. Try to exclude artificial lights, such as streetlights or lighted windows, as these will burn out in the image. You will also need to use a tripod and experiment with a very long shutter speed – maybe several minutes. The result will look like daylight except the colors will be subtly different. And if you can include areas of movement – the surface of a lake, the sea, tree branches – the result will be particularly eye-catching.

Get it in black and white

Winter, with its endless succession of grim gray days, may seem like a bad time for landscape photography. Color pictures taken under these conditions often look flat and dull.

This is where you can go back in time, and take black and white (B&W) photographs (also called 'monochrome' or 'grayscale'). The dramatic light of a winter's day could give you some strong stuff. Alternatively, rain can add an element of softness and tranquility to a scene. And if there is a strong wind blowing, by using a slow shutter speed you will blur grass and branches for an effect similar to the one with running water (See 'Go with the flow'). Just make sure your camera is firmly supported again. You don't want the whole landscape blurred.

There are two ways of taking B&W photographs with a digital camera:

1. By setting your camera to the 'Monochrome' ('Grayscale') option so that the photograph is taken in black and white, in camera.

2. Taking a color photograph and converting it to grayscale with your image editing program back at the computer.

This is one occasion when 'getting it right in the camera' doesn't apply. In general the second option is a far better one. It gives you more control over the final image and, if ever you want the color, it is there in the original. If you take the photograph in monochrome to start with, there is no possibility of retrieving the color.

There are various ways of converting a color image to grayscale at your computer. The simplest will be to click the 'Grayscale' option in the Edit menu and – hey presto! – the job is done. A more sophisticated way, which gives better control, is to use the 'Channel Mixer', 'Levels' and 'Curves' options of your image-processing program. Details of how to do this are

Opposite: Photographs don't have to be brightly-colored. Monochrome often works well. The lack of color in this scene adds to the bleak feeling.

given in more advanced photographic books, and tutorials are regularly carried in the pages of photo magazines.

If you are photographing in lousy weather, make sure your built-in flash is turned off. If the light is dim and your flash is on automatic, it may well fire. Not only is this useless for a landscape, it will ruin the image by giving the wrong exposure. And, if there is mist about, the flash will reflect off the water droplets in the air, completely ruining the contrast.

On your bike

If you can manage it, scout for good landscapes on your bicycle. This will enable you to cover more ground than on foot but, at the same time, you will be closer to the scenery than in a car. On top of that, you will also be able to get to places inaccessible to cars. Then, when you find a good view, and want to investigate more closely, a bike is much easier to park than a car. Finally, it will help to keep you fit. A mountain bike is best for this, with your gear carried in a backpack.

Boots 'n all

Accessories for landscape photography go beyond lenses. Don't forget to take boots as well. Or, better still, get some waders. They will allow you to find new and interesting viewpoints. Think of the stunning image you could get if you can stand a little way out in a calm, mirror-still lake and take a picture with the camera almost at water level.

Dressing up

Don't neglect your clothing, either. Pursuing that perfect landscape will take you to some wild and windy spots, at some cold times of day. Hypothermia can seriously affect your photographic skills.

The best technique is to dress in layers – a base layer such as a thermal vest, then a shirt, on top of that something like a fleece and, finally, an outer wind and waterproof layer. In that way you can control your temperature precisely, shedding layers if you get too hot, or putting them back on when you are standing still, waiting for the light.

It's in the bag

And don't forget foul-weather gear for your camera. A supply of clear plastic bags a little bigger than your camera, and elastic bands, will be perfect.

When the rain descends on you, as it surely will, put your camera in the bag and, using the elastic band, fasten the mouth of the bag securely around the lens barrel, as close to the end as possible. Provided your bag isn't torn, this set-up will provide perfect waterproofing whilst still allowing you to use all the camera controls.

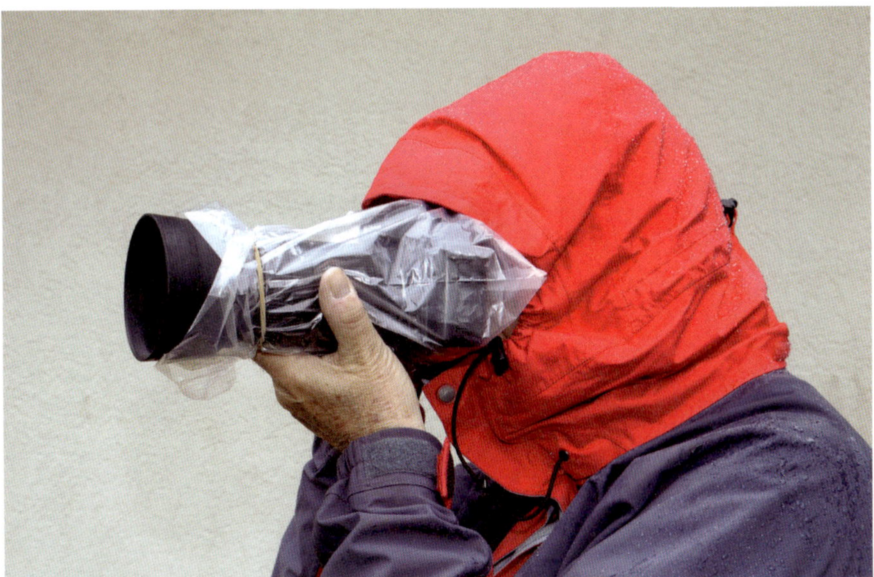

A plastic bag over the camera gives good protection. Don't worry what it looks like, the camera stays dry.

At a push, you can also fill one of the bags with air, seal it and use it as a
steadying cushion.

QUICK T!P

If you are going to a remote place to get that stunning landscape, inform
someone of your expected time of return. And carry a whistle and a mobile
phone, just in case.

DID YOU KNOW ...

'Chimping' is a derogatory term used by some professional
photographers to describe the way in which people look at every
image on the camera screen, going "Ooooh!" and "Aaahhh!". But,
by looking at your images you're seeing if they're coming out right.
So, chimp on!

'Bokeh' (pronounced "bo" as in botox and "ke" as in Kenya)
is a word referring to the appearance of out-of-focus areas in a
photograph.

The item that has been requested more than any other from the
US National Archives is a photograph of Elvis Presley and Richard M.
Nixon shaking hands on the occasion of Presley's visit to the White
House on December 21, 1970.

A limited edition Leica M7 camera was sold for a world record price
of €90,000, a world record for a modern camera. The original
owner, photographer Sebastiao Saldago, was given the camera in
2005, in recognition of his humanistic work. He used the money
raised by the camera to preserve 120,000 trees in the rainforests of
his native Brazil.

The first true zoom lens, which remained in focus while the focal
length of the lens assembly was changed, was patented in the US
1902 by Clile C. Allen.

Chapter summary

- Start landscape photography with a familiar place. You will know the various viewpoints and how it looks under different weather conditions.

- Watch the weather forecast and plan your trips.

- Get up early, or stay out late, for the best light.

- Make sure every landscape has a subject.

- Include some foreground.

- Use a polarizing filter to enhance colors, especially the sky.

- For the best panoramas, mount your camera on a tripod and make sure it's level.

- If there is too much light difference between the sky and the land, use a graduated neutral density filter.

- Try creating dramatic landscapes with monochrome, but do it at the computer. Take the photographs in color.

- Dress up well when going to remote places, and take safety precautions.

If a picture's not good enough, you weren't close enough.

Robert Capa

Be a Good Sport

Chapter 7

Be a Good Sport

You don't need to go to the Yankee Stadium or Center Court at Wimbledon to get stunning sports images. In fact, it may be better if you don't. At the big sporting venues, you're likely to be up in the crowd, a long way from the action, with no space to steady your camera and people leaping up and down in front of you every time something happens.

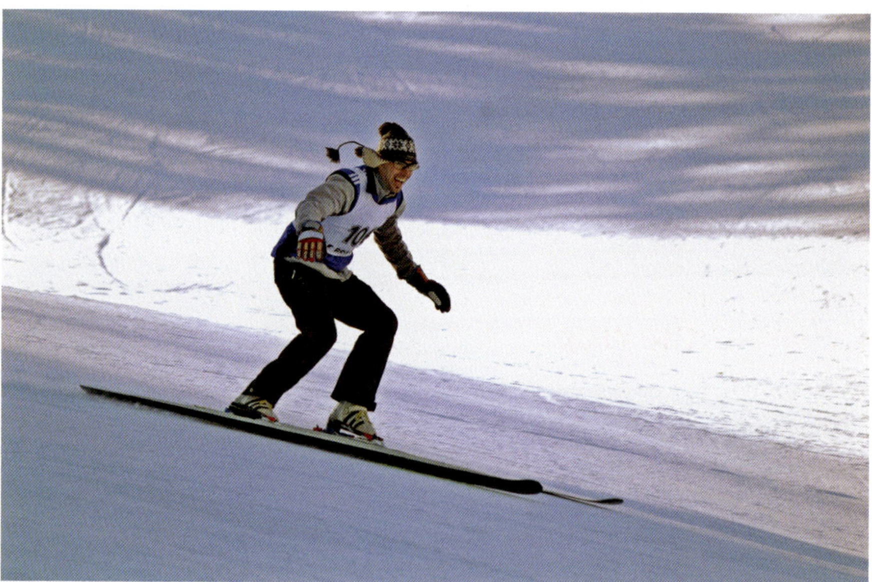

Competitors in amateur events have great fun, and can give better photo-opportunities.

Don't worry. There is plenty of sport right on your doorstep. Local clubs – football, basketball, tennis, athletics and more – are packed with wannabees who, evenings and weekends, give heart and soul in competition. Go local, get close to the action, and try these tips …

I'm converted!

You don't necessarily need a lens like a small artillery piece to get action shots. If you can't afford a huge telephoto lens, use a teleconverter.

Teleconverters will only work on cameras with interchangeable lenses. They fit between the camera body and the main lens, and increase its focal length by a fixed amount, usually 1.4 or 2 times. For example, if you put a 1.4 converter on a 100mm lens it will become a 140mm lens.

But, as usual, there is a price to pay. A teleconverter is an extra chunk of glass, so it may affect the quality of your image slightly. A more important disadvantage is that it will lower the speed of your lens. A 1.4× teleconverter gives a loss of one stop, and a 2× one gives a loss of two stops. A 'two stop' reduction means you will have to slow the shutter speed by two 'clicks' (e.g. from 1/250th sec to 1/60th sec) to maintain the correct exposure, and that is a significant reduction when you're shooting action shots.

Cream of the crop

If you don't want to use a teleconverter, another approach is to get as close to the action as you can and then, when you are processing your photos on your computer, cut out all the extraneous stuff and home in on the action. This is called cropping. The professionals do it too … in spite of their massive lenses.

But, the downside of cropping is that you're reducing the image size.

When cropping an image always save it with a different filename. That way you always retain the full-sized original.

At the bitter end

When photographing football, basketball or similar sports, try to position yourself at the end of the pitch or the court, so the players are running towards you. Their relative motion will be less of a problem, and you are more likely to catch the ball in your image. You'll also be right on the spot when a team scores.

You'll have to accept, assuming the teams are evenly matched, that you are going to miss about half of the action. And if they're not evenly matched, get to the losing team's end – fast. (That's another advantage of going local – you can usually shift position easily.)

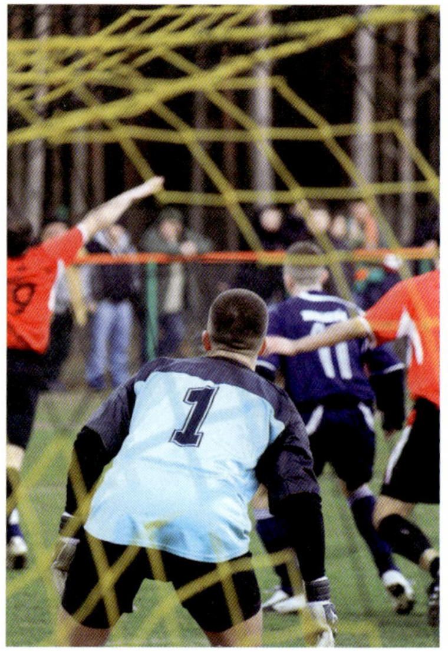

Even standing right behind the goal can give you some dramatic action shots.

If you do shift position and you're covering an outdoor sport, take note of where the sun is. You don't want to be facing directly into it and risk your pictures being washed out by lens flare.

A bit on the side

Another way to get close-ups of the action is to think laterally … lateral to the sports ground, that is.

In certain sports (e.g. horse riding, gymnastics, martial arts) there are often areas to one side where competitors practice, warm up or cool off. Access to these areas tends to be more open and you can often get close to the participants. Whilst they may not be in the full 'heat' of competition, they will still be trying hard and practicing all the moves, so you'll have an opportunity for excellent shots.

If you see it … you've missed it

In most sports, the action happens in milliseconds.

So the key to success is timing. To get the best shots you have to be familiar with what is going to happen, pressing the shutter button an instant before the 'bat hits ball'. If you see the strike, you've missed the picture.

To increase your chances, hold the shutter button half way down, so the camera has focused and done its exposure 'thing', then press it all the way an instant before the crucial moment. Apart from that, there is no other easy way around this. It is practice, practice, practice.

Bursting blues

Some cameras have 'burst mode' in which they can take 3-4 shots per second and you may think that this is the answer to the timing problem. Switch it on, hold down the shutter button and … pow! … pow! … pow! … you're sure to capture the action, aren't you?

Not necessarily.

Do the math. If a crucial moment of action – like the bat hitting the ball – lasts 1/30th of a second (which is a generous assumption) and you're taking pictures at 3 shots per second, you only have a 1 in 10 chance of catching it perfectly.

And another disadvantage of burst mode is that, when the camera has taken its 3 or 4 shots, it locks up while it records them on the memory card.

This may take a second or so, time in which something else dramatic, like a catch, can happen.

For these reasons many professional sports photographers (even with top-of-the-range cameras that can get 10 shots per second) do not use 'burst mode'. There is still no mechanical substitute for the human eye, anticipation, and human reactions.

Let's get this in focus

It is no use capturing the crucial moment of action if your subjects are out of focus. Unfortunately most autofocus systems are too slow to handle the rapidly changing distances that you'll find in sports events.

There are two ways around this. Switch off your autofocus and use either 'zone focus' or 'follow focus'.

In zone focus you pre-set the focus to a certain important area where you are pretty sure some action is going to take place (the basket in basketball, for example) and leave it set there.

Follow focus is better for sports, such as running, where the competitors move on predictable paths at relatively steady speeds. With one hand you rotate the focus ring smoothly to keep your subject sharp. Some single lens reflex cameras even have an autofocus setting which will do this automatically (sometimes called 'continuous focus'). However, this is not always infallible.

It's the folks who count

Sport is about people. Watch them. Look for expressions of mental or physical anguish on their faces. Certain players may regularly display bouts of anger, passion or just plain craziness. Others are amazingly agile. Some may regularly do victory dances. Follow them for the best and most dramatic shots.

And don't only photograph the winners. The anguish or exhaustion of the losers can make equally dramatic images.

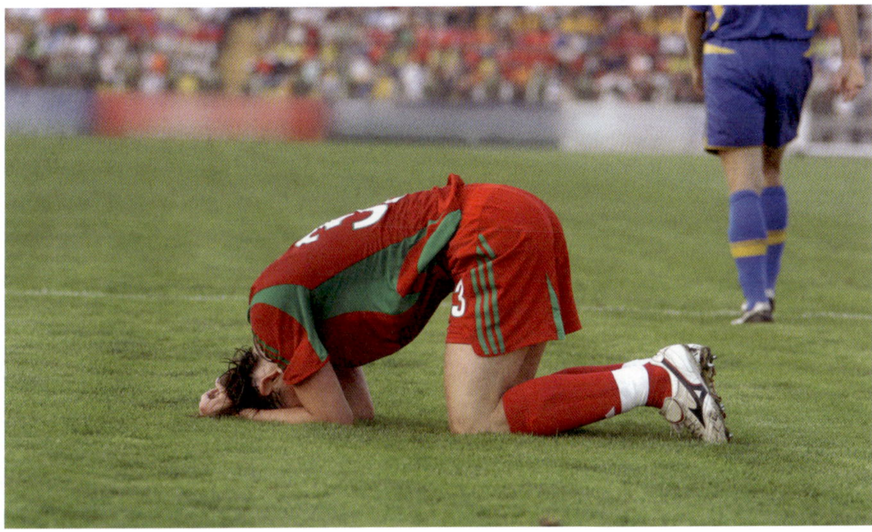

Even when the action is over there are still opportunities for great photographs.

QUICK T!P

Watch the spectators, too. They can be a source of more great shots.

Panning for gold

For most sports you want to use the highest shutter speed possible in order to freeze the action. So crank it up to over 1/500th second if you can.

But sometimes you don't want it all sharp. For example, if you photograph motor racing using a high shutter speed the cars will look as if they're parked on the track.

Try panning instead.

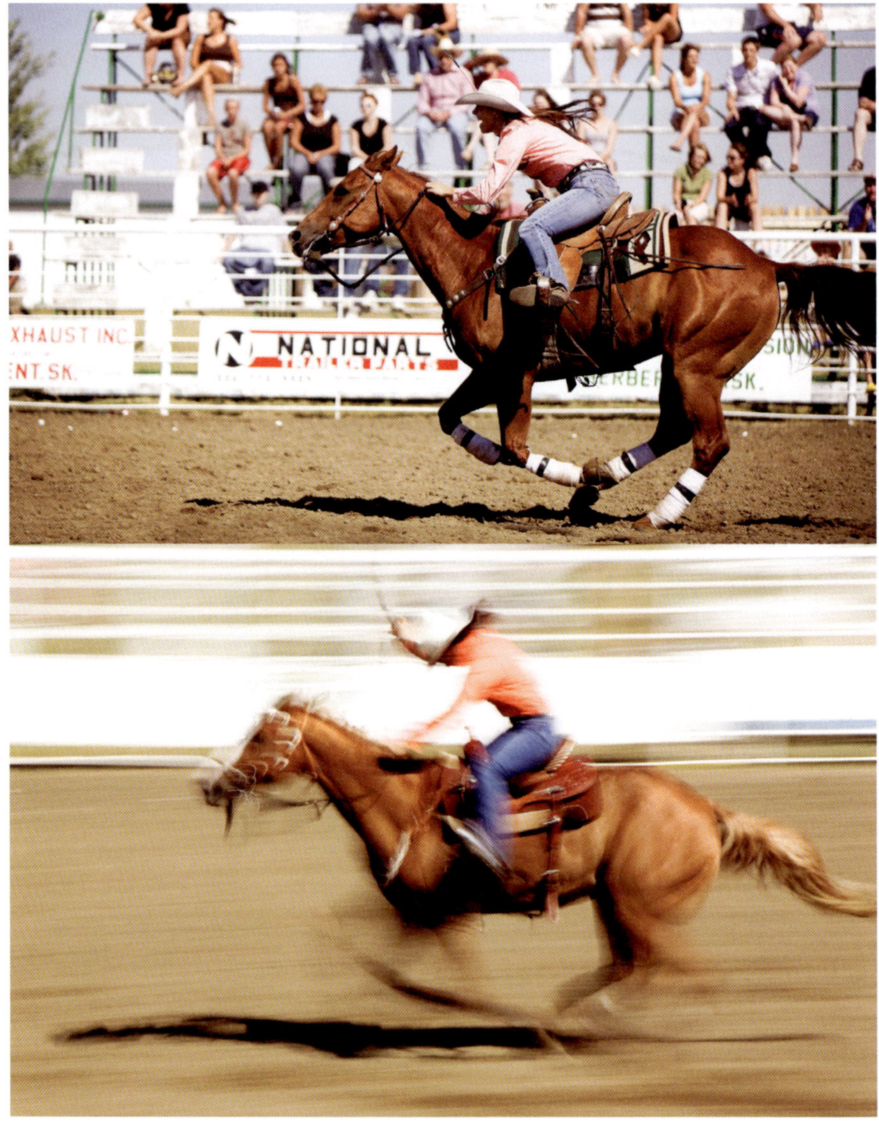

Top: At a high shutter speed the action is frozen and the background is sharp, which can detract from the image.

Bottom: Using a slower shutter speed gives an impression of speed, and blurs the background too, making the action stand out.

Panning is the technique of swinging around to follow the subject whilst using a relatively slow shutter speed. This blurs the background into a series of streaks giving a sense of speed. It also blurs moving parts, like wheels.

In motor racing, for example, position yourself on a corner, or a technically demanding part of the track, where the cars will be traveling more slowly. Start with a shutter speed of 1/60 sec, but if you find the results too blurred, move up to 1/125. Don't go above this speed. Switch off the autofocus and focus on a spot where the cars will be closest. Then swing around smoothly with each passing car, keeping it in the same position in your viewfinder. Press the shutter when it passes your pre-arranged 'focus spot'. Keep trying. Practice makes perfect.

The lowest of the low

If you can manage it, get down to the same level as the action, or lower. For example, if you are taking pictures of marathon runners, try photographing them from ground level.

This has two advantages. First, it brings your viewer right into the action. Second, it usually simplifies the background. By getting low you can often get the competitors against the sky, which greatly increases the drama.

Overleaf: The low viewpoint adds to the sense of action and has the added benefit of highlighting the runners against the sky.

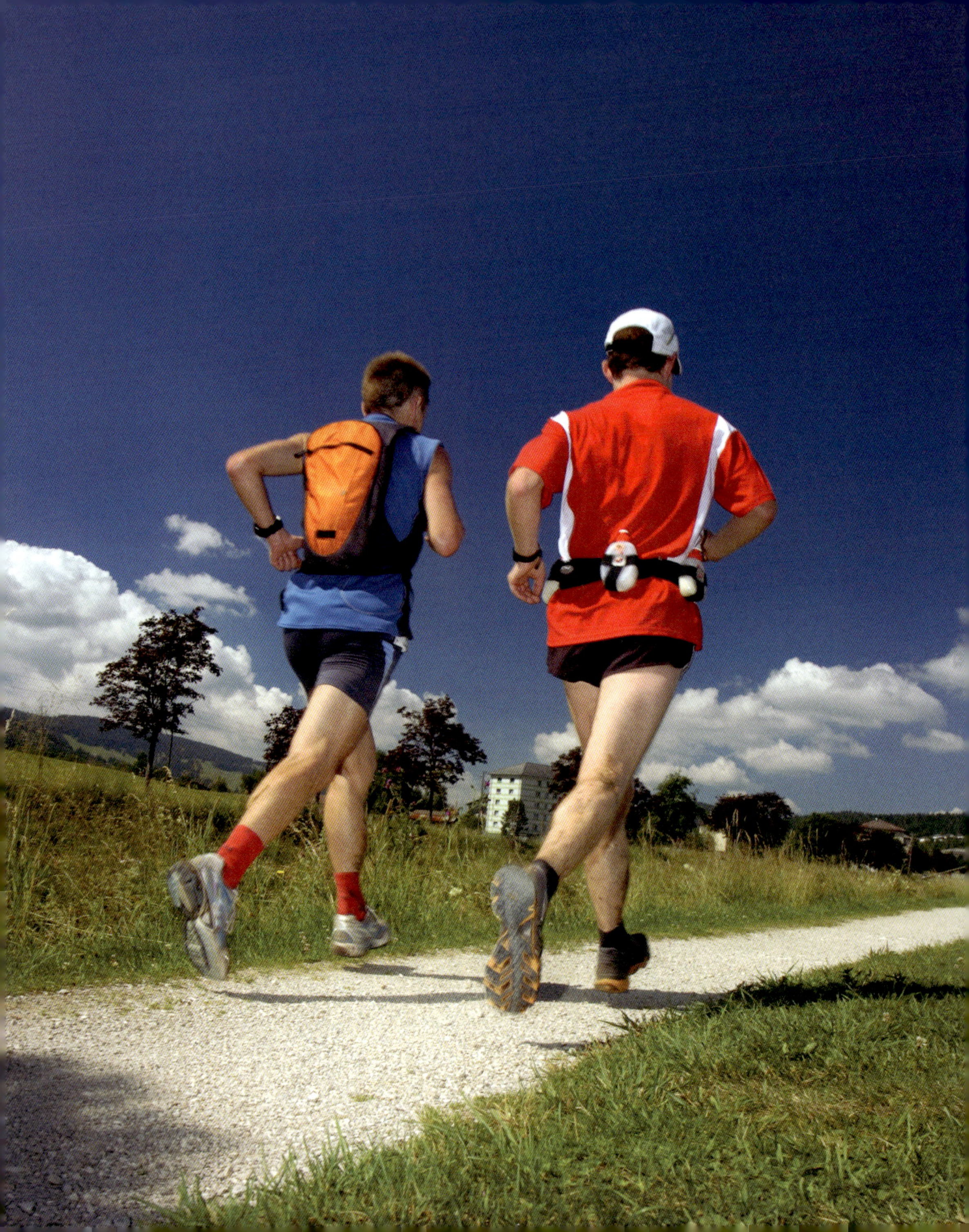

Memory overload

Be ready for a whole heap of dud shots when photographing sports. So take plenty. With digital cameras they cost nothing. The more photographs you take, the more likely you are to capture that brilliant one. It is not unusual for professionals to take hundreds of shots and then only use one or two.

But then you could well find you're beginning to run short of memory. If this happens, use breaks in the action to scroll through your images on the camera's rear screen and erase the ones where you've only caught half an arm and a leg.

QUICK T!P

When checking your images, remember that viewing the screen drains the battery rapidly.

Insurance shots

Take a few general photos for 'insurance' in case none of your action shots come out – subjects like a tennis player serving, runners lined up at the start or kick-off in a soccer match.

Then, at half time, or in a break between races, look for other photographic opportunities. There will be plenty … the equipment that's used, the markings on the track, exhausted competitors or weirdly-dressed spectators. Even if you do get the most brilliant action shots, these more mundane ones won't be wasted. They'll provide context for your portfolio.

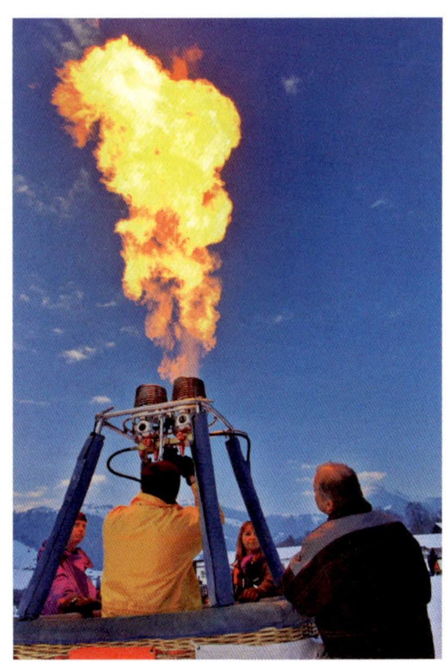

You can find drama and color, even before the balloon goes up.

Make yourself known

Before starting to photograph any sport, it's a good idea to introduce yourself to the organizers. And this is especially important if the sport involves children … even if they're your own.

Not only will the organizers appreciate the fact that you've let them know you'll be there, you may even get a few commissions, print sales, or permission to get closer to the action … all from just one polite conversation.

Anyone for wife-carrying?

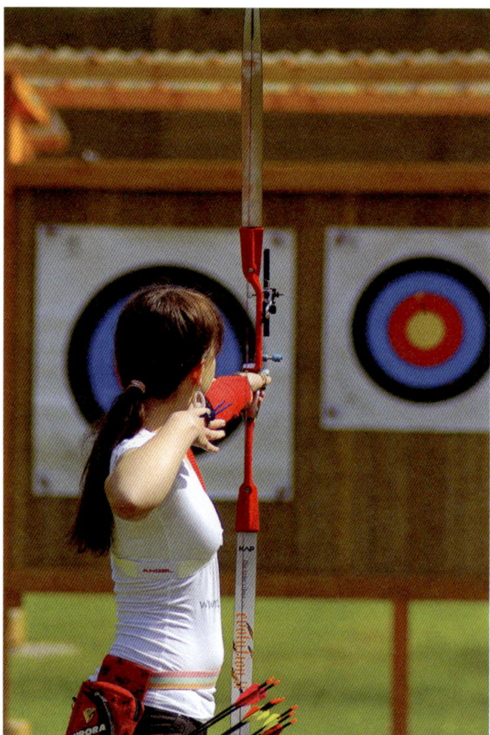

When it comes to sports, don't just think of the big ones like baseball, tennis or athletics. Plenty of excellent photographic opportunities exist in less well-known sports. How about croquet, fencing or archery?

Then you could try the bizarre. How about cow chip throwing? … snail racing? … wife-carrying? Search the internet or look at local papers. You could find some wildly off-beat events taking place in your region.

On target. Archery is a long-range sport. But with a careful choice of viewpoint you can get it all in.

Chapter summary

- Unless you have a press pass, there are much better photo opportunities at local events than at national ones.

- Use a teleconverter to increase the focal length of your lens.

- Stand at one of the ends when photographing team sports played on a pitch.

- Anticipate the action and fire the shutter an instant before.

- Don't rely on 'burst mode' to capture the crucial moment.

- Don't rely on autofocus either. Use 'zone focus' or 'follow focus'.

- With sports involving rapid side-to-side movement, try panning.

- Get down to the level of the action.

- Introduce yourself to the organizers.

- Look out for unusual sports, too.

> *"There are always two people in every picture: the photographer and the viewer."*

Ansel Adams

Child's Play? No Way!

Chapter 8

Child's Play? No Way!

Let's get one thing straight. Photographing toddlers and children is not child's play! You point your camera … and little Freda hides, pouts, or bursts into tears. What you thought was going to be a walkover turns out to be a hue and cry.

To get the best shots of children you'll need running shoes coupled with a little knowledge and low cunning. The underlying principle is to get the kids used to being photographed. It is also important to choose your time. No one likes having their photo taken when they are tired or hungry, especially young children.

So, to get good photographs of children you must become a high-speed, cunning psychologist.

And use these tips …

Fire away

As with sports photography, be prepared to take lots and lots of photographs of kids to get a few good ones. In this field, if you take 100 pictures and get 10 excellent ones, you're doing well.

Babes in arms

It can be difficult to get good portraits of newborn babies because they are much too young to do anything but lie in their cots with a blank expression (unless they get a bout of wind, when it can look as if they are smiling).

Of course, you want a record of your child in the earliest months, but an alternative approach is to take photos of other body parts. How about a close-up of a tiny hand grasping dad's great big one? Or ten tiny toes, with Mum playing 'This Little Piggy?'

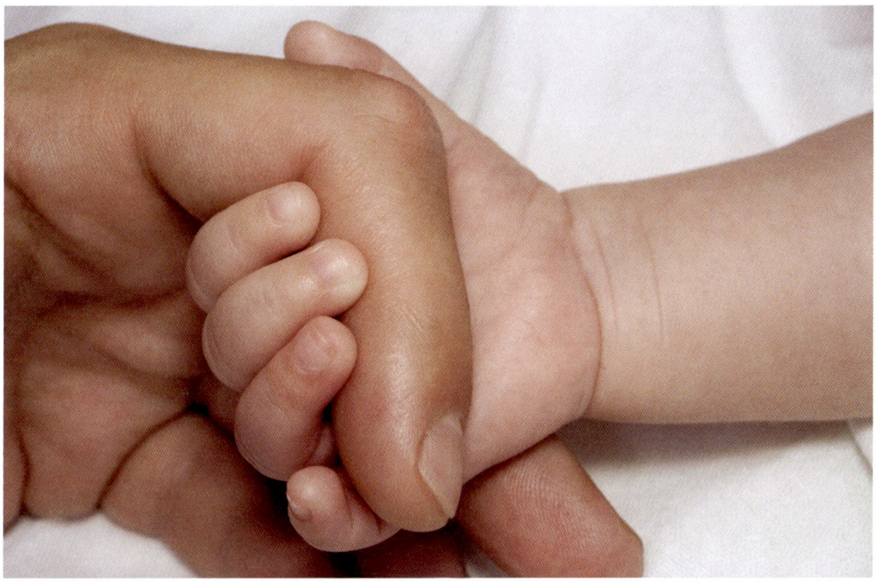

Close-ups work well with newborn babies.

Getting up close accentuates the detail.

Mum's the word … or dad

Slightly older babies won't pose, or smile to order either … unless you apply a little psychology. Babies are at their happiest when they're with their parents, so use mum or dad. Get one (or both) to interact with baby, off-camera. They could play with a favorite toy, pull funny faces or sing a nursery rhyme, just out of sight of the lens. Then your subject will break out in an angelic smile.

Overleaf: Mum off-camera does the trick, bringing out this beautiful smile.

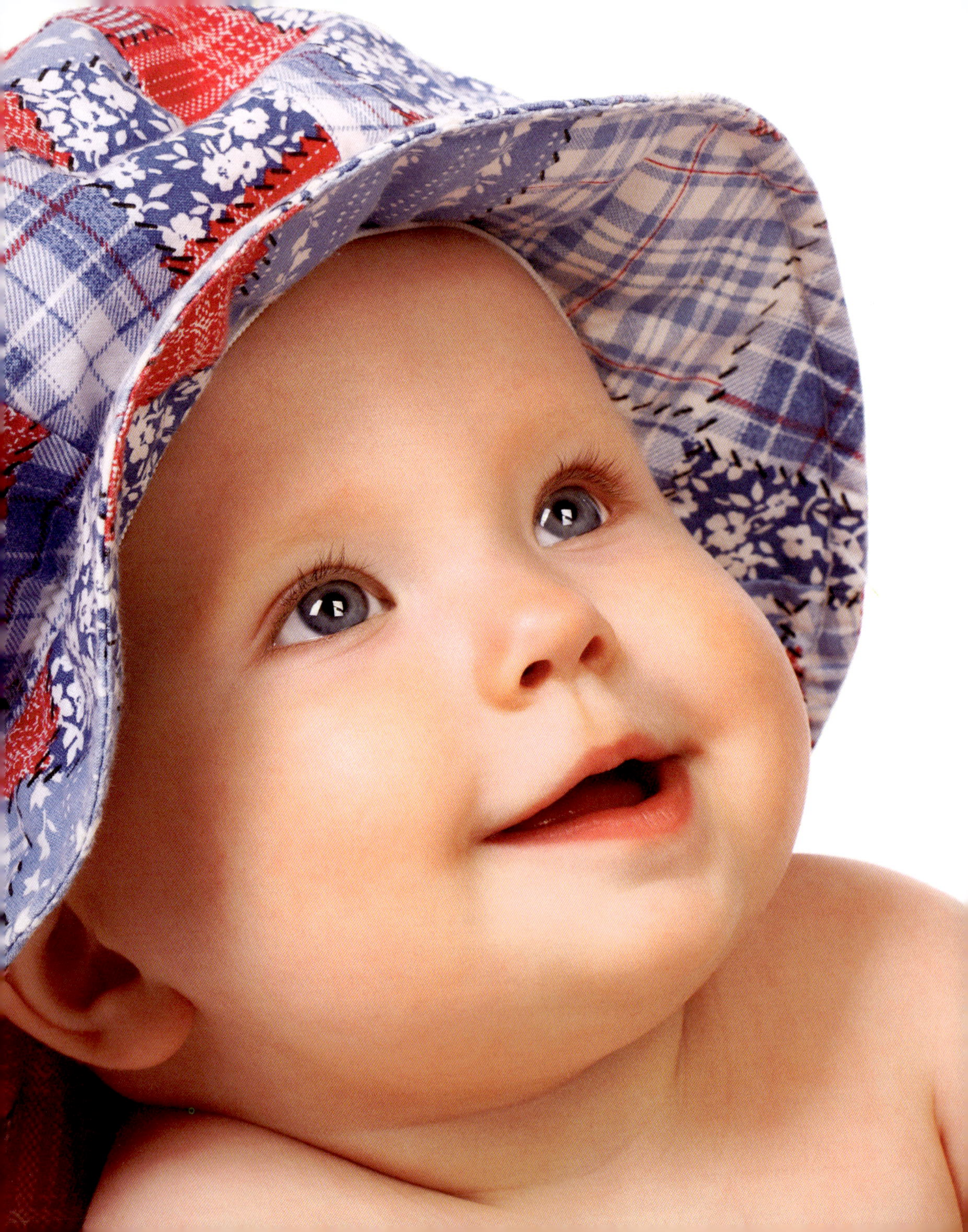

Don't hide

If you crouch behind the camera looking through the viewfinder your face will be hidden. This can be frightening for babies and toddlers. All they see is a single 'eye' looking at them. A better technique is to put the camera on a tripod, frame and focus it on the child, and then stand beside it using a remote release to take the pictures.

Follow-my-leader

"Sit still. Smile. Mummy wants a nice piccy," won't cut the mustard with older children, either. Trying to pose them formally can be frustrating. And the danger is, the harder you try, the more out-of-control the situation can get.

So forget the formal poses. They look stilted anyway. Turn kids' energy and inquisitiveness to your advantage. Let them do what they want and discreetly follow them around (in your running shoes). Better still, take them somewhere interesting, to the woods, a sand-pit, or a stream. They will become so absorbed with the possibilities of their new environment that they will ignore you. You'll be able to capture them exploring, adventuring and making new discoveries.

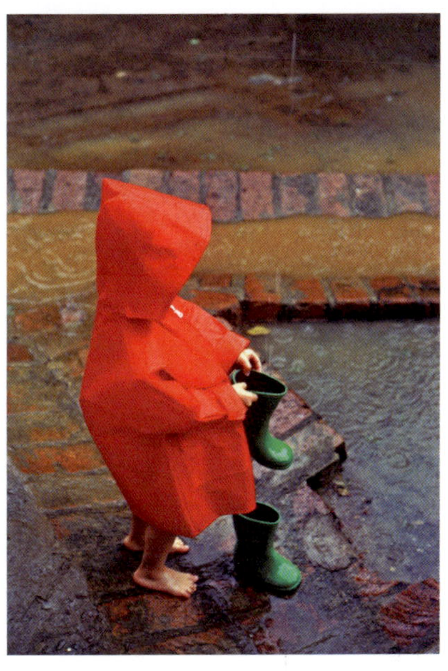

Water and wellies. Who could want more? In this case a high viewpoint works, isolating the subject against a neutral background.

QUICK T!P

Another approach is to ask the children how *they* want to be photographed. Draw them into the process. Let them call the shots.

Dressing down

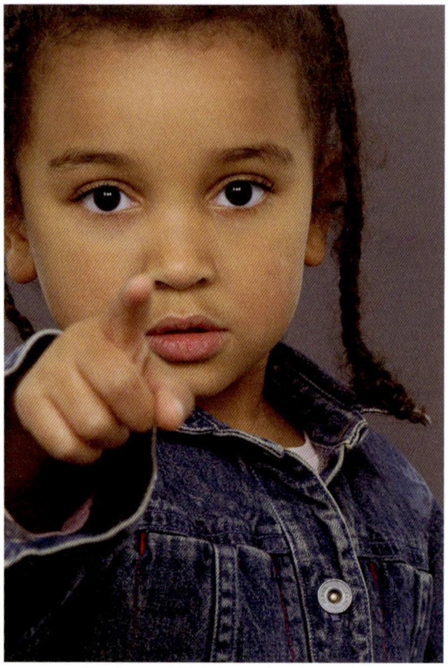

Denim adds punch to this active portrait.

Children don't have to be photographed in their best clothes. In many ways it is better if they aren't dolled up to the nines. Then they are free to muck about, giving you the opportunity for those brilliant informal shots.

As for choice of colors, plain ones are best. Avoid large or bold patterns such as checks, stripes or spots and dots. Avoid clothing with wording on it, too. All these things draw attention away from the child's face, which is the most important part of the photo.

QUICK T!P

Denim is one of the best materials for a photography session. It's hard-wearing, neutral and comes out beautifully on photographs, whether you're using color or black and white.

Propped up

If you can't get out and about … it's a lousy winter's day for example … then try giving children something to play with. Dressing-up clothes work wonders, as do a few simple props. For example, an upturned table can be a pirate's galleon, a big old bus or a spacecraft. Get them to play pirates, bus-drivers or astronauts.

Opposite: The low viewpoint increases the impact of this image. Pity the eye patch is upside down!

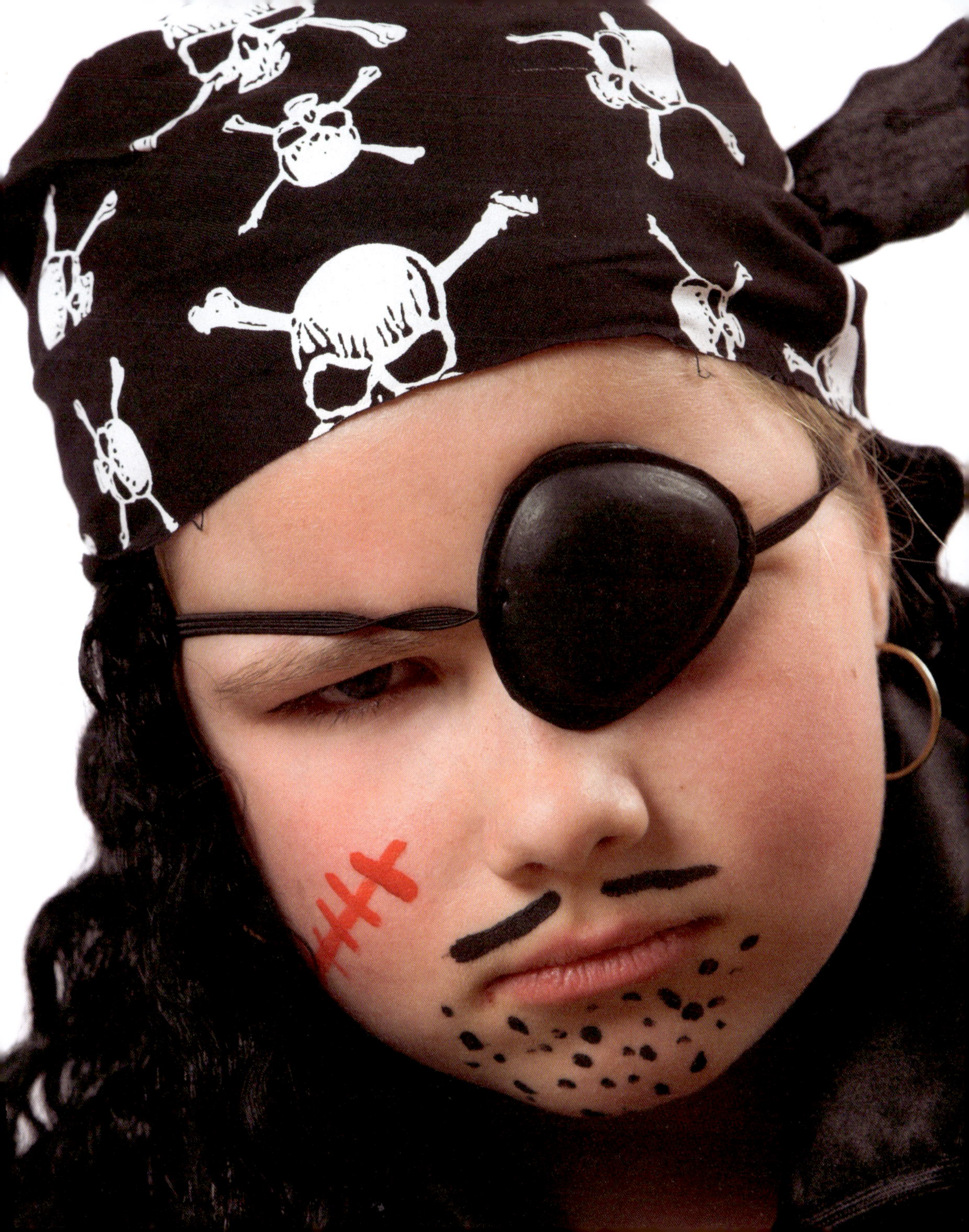

Trick or treat

But sometimes you want your children to be photographed in a more formal pose.

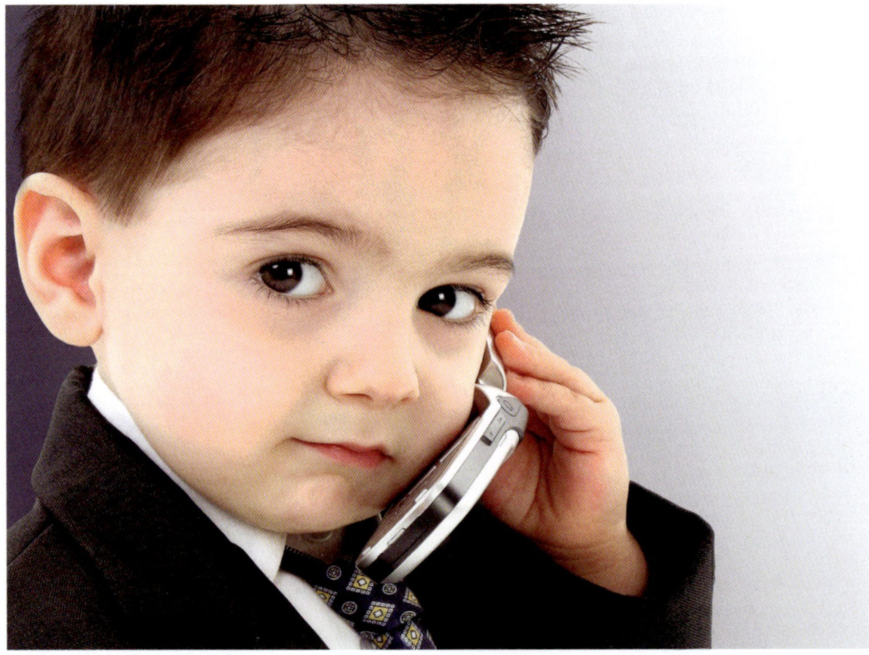

Small props don't have to be toys. Something from adult life can work wonders too.

Okay. Then don't just plonk them down on a seat and expect them to smile sweetly to order. They're more likely to be frowning with frustration. Having some tricks up your sleeve may solve the problem. Some ideas that work are:

a.   Engaging them in a conversation, asking simple questions that they can answer.

b.   Playing word games (like 'I Spy') suited to the age of the child.

c.   Singing a song or nursery rhyme together.

d.   Giving them a small new toy to play with.

e.   Blowing bubbles.

Techniques like these are far better than bribing children with candy. Candies are messy, unhealthy and make for horribly sticky mouths and strange facial expressions.

Get down, get down, get down

When photographing children get down to their level. Photos taken from above will have a distorted look. Meet children eye-to-eye.

Getting down to their level, and smiling, also helps you connect with young children. A large person towering over a child, wielding all sorts of strange equipment, can be intimidating.

Party popper

When little Freda's birthday party comes around you'll want a lot of photos. Make sure you take some before the party begins. That's when she will be looking her best, before the ice-cream gets spilt and the arguments erupt.

She is also more likely to pose sweetly. You can work beside a window for wonderful soft light, or next to the birthday cake (still in one piece!). And, as an added bonus, you will be able to work out the correct settings for bounce flash, whether there will be any unsightly reflections, or the best position for a neutral background, all before the action heats up.

Overleaf: Before the party begins the smile is still happy and excited, the lighting is soft, and the cake is all in one piece.

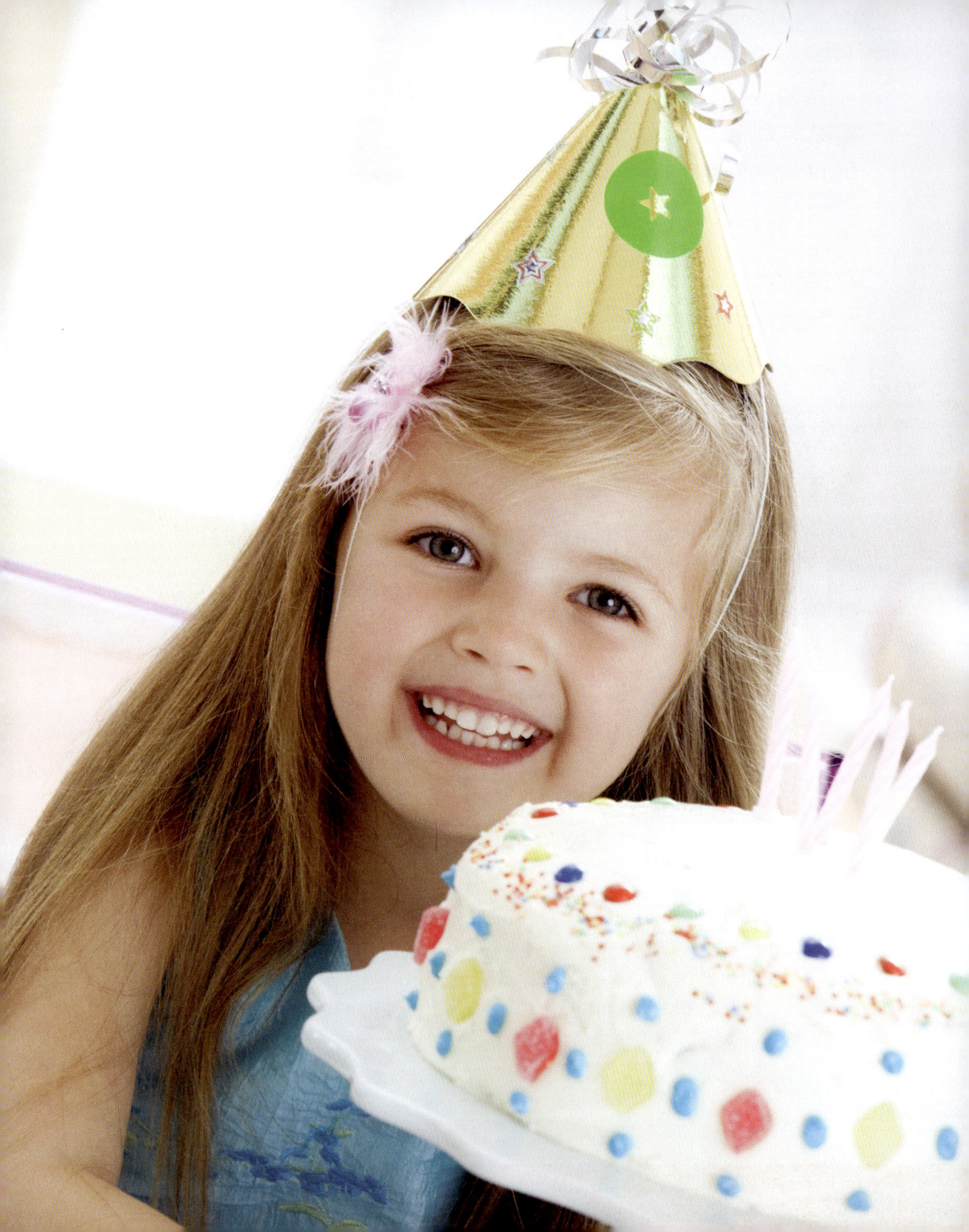

Who's taking the pictures here?

If you can make a photo-session fun you are much more likely to get good images. So, how about switching roles from time to time? Let little Freda take a picture of *you*.

You don't have to let her run off with your expensive camera. You can hold it at arm's length and let her push the button. Or, better still, if you have a cheap compact camera you could let her play with that.

Teenage torment

Photographing teenagers can be as difficult as photographing small children … for different reasons. Time for more psychology. Teenagers love to feel mature and you can use this to your advantage.

Don't tell them that you want to take their picture. Ask them if they want to be a model and show off their latest gear. They'll know what's hot and what's not. All you'll need to do is find the setting. As usual, clean uncluttered backgrounds work best.

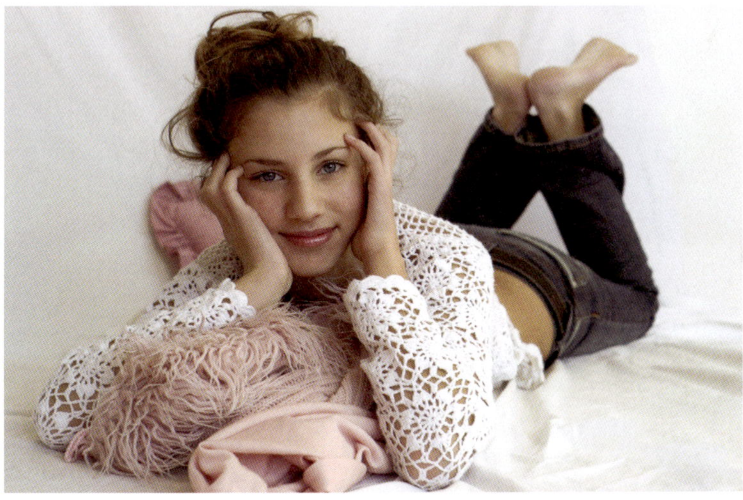

Take another tack with a teen.

And, when you're totally exhausted …

… take the easy way out. Photograph the little darlings when they're asleep. In fact, do this anyway. Children look beautifully peaceful and content when they're sleeping.

Don't use flash as it tends to give a harsh light and the brilliant burst of bright light may wake them. Use a tripod and a slow shutter speed. They won't be moving much. And if you want a warm feel to the image, switch on a bedside lamp.

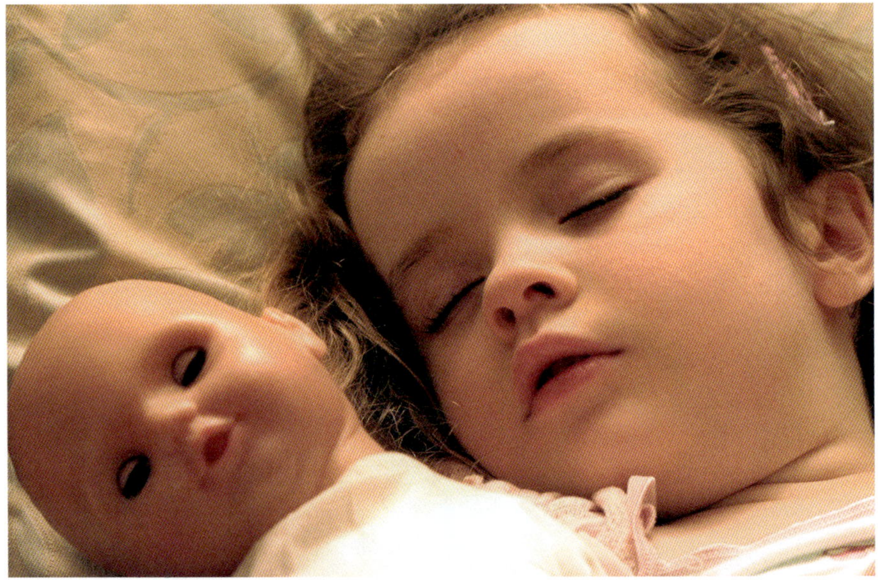

And when you're too exhausted to chase them any more …

Chapter summary

- Be ready to take lots and lots of photographs for a few good ones.

- Take close-ups of hands and feet with newborn babies.

- Use mum and dad to generate beautiful smiles in babies.

- When photographing toddlers, don't hide behind the camera. It can scare them.

- Turn children's energy to your advantage. Give them an interesting environment.

- Dress children down for photographs. Avoid bold patterns or clothes with words. Denim is good.

- If you want a formal pose, engage the child in conversation, singing, story-telling.

- When photographing birthday parties, take shots before the party begins.

- Use teenagers' fashion sense to help in posing them.

- Photograph children when they're asleep.

"I really believe that there are things that nobody would see if I didn't photograph them."

Diane Arbus

High Days … Holidays … Houses … and Other Things …

Chapter 9

High Days … Holidays … Houses … and Other Things …

Off the beach

When on holiday, don't just take the same old pictures of the family on the beach … family in the restaurant … family at the amusement park. Include some that capture the essence of your destination too. Look out for its landscapes, climate, architecture, signs, culture and so on. Also find out when the local markets are held, or if there are any festivals taking place. These can provide fabulous opportunities for colorful and unusual photographs.

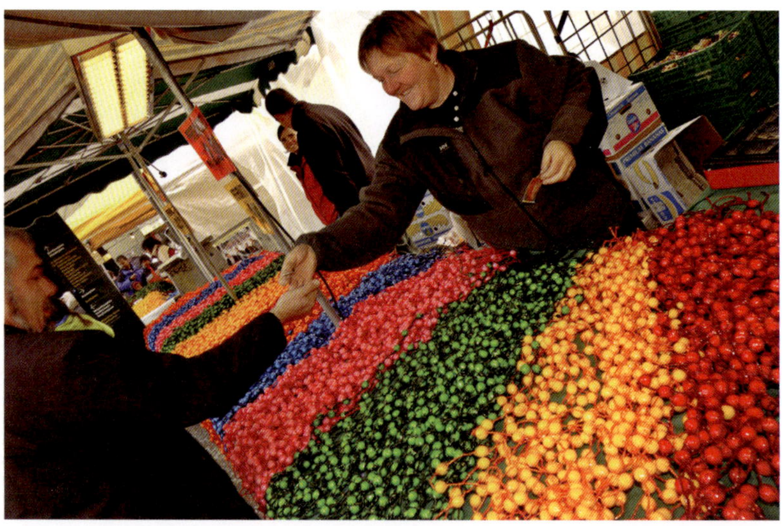

The money changing hands turns this colorful market shot into a small story.

Be the same – but different

When on holiday you can get lots of ideas for local landscape photos by looking at postcards, tourist brochures, or talking to taxi drivers. But then, having found a famous location, try to find a different viewpoint if you can. Going that little bit further can change a good photograph into a great one.

When you're on holiday, ask your hotel manager if you can go up on to the roof, at sunrise or sunset. You'll get some unique images from there.

People who need people

When traveling, be careful about photographing local people. Try to chat with them first and obtain their permission. One excellent way of breaking the ice is to show them the photographs you've taken on the camera screen. Offer to send them copies. Once you have established a rapport, they may let you photograph freely.

But, also be aware that in many countries the laws with regard to photographing in public places may be different from those in your home country. Find out what's acceptable and what's not before you go.

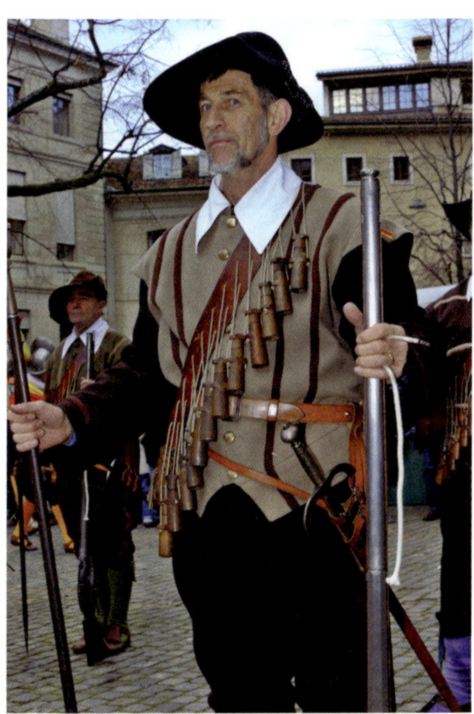

You can also photograph people in traditional ceremonies, like here, at the annual 'Escalade' festival in Geneva, Switzerland.

Tell a story

Photograph the stories that go with your holiday, too – packing, getting lost, buying souvenirs, admiring a view. Such images work much better than the same old shots of everyone standing in a line in front of some tourist attraction. But try to photograph candidly wherever possible as it looks more natural than posed photos.

Hang about

If you're on a day trip to a remote location – say to an island – it's often a good idea to hang about behind for a little while when you get off the boat. Everyone else will rush off to see the sights leaving you in a tranquil and peaceful spot. Local wildlife, such as the birds, may well come down if you're still and quiet. You don't have to stay there. Move on when the rest of the tour party has spread out a bit. In that way you'll be lagging behind a little. You'll find places more empty, and you're more likely to get natural photographs.

On parade

When photographing parades, don't over-burden yourself with kit. Try to use only one lens, such as a 70–300mm telephoto. Although the cortege may be slow-moving, changing lenses will still waste time and you may miss great shots.

Get to the location of the parade early and find a good spot at the beginning of the route. The marchers will be fresh there, and responding to the crowd. At the end they'll probably be hot, tired and fed up.

Because of the crowds, a tripod will probably be out of the question. You'll be hand-holding. So set your camera to aperture priority, at maximum aperture. That will consistently give the highest shutter-speed for the light conditions whilst throwing the faces on the far side of the road out of focus (remember your depth of field?).

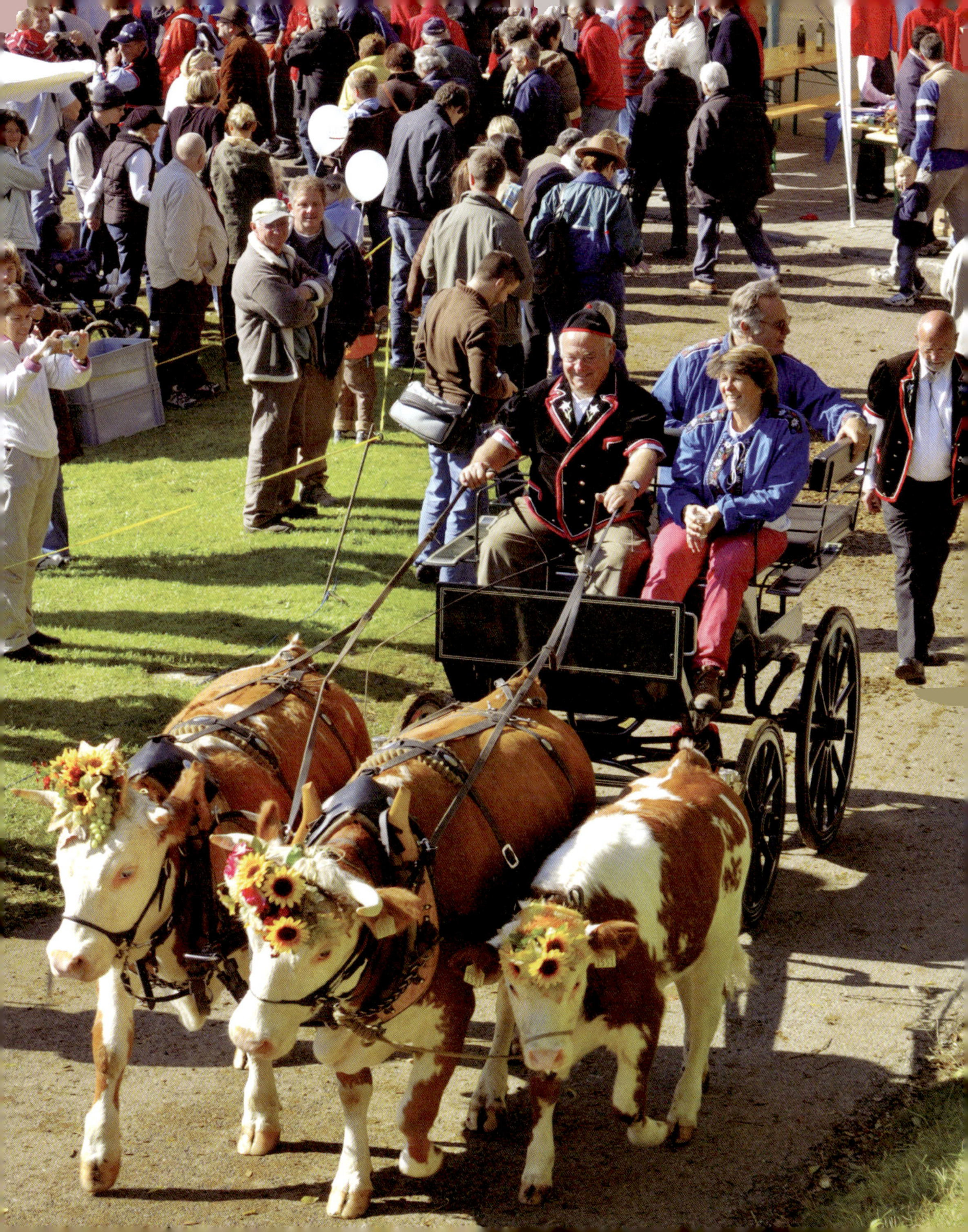

Another approach is to find a shooting spot higher up – on a wall, plinth of a fountain, or even up a tree. Not only will this give you a better view, it will also help reduce the background clutter.

Architecture

There are some stunning buildings around but, as with landscapes, getting them to look good on photographs can be tough.

Forget about trying to cram everything in. Instead, home in on the detail – pipework, a leering gargoyle, or the texture of brickwork.

Another problem is something called 'converging verticals'. Most often, when you're photographing a building, the only place to stand is at the base, looking up. Your eye subconsciously corrects what you see, but the camera doesn't. So, in the photo all the vertical lines converge, making it look as if the building is falling over backwards.

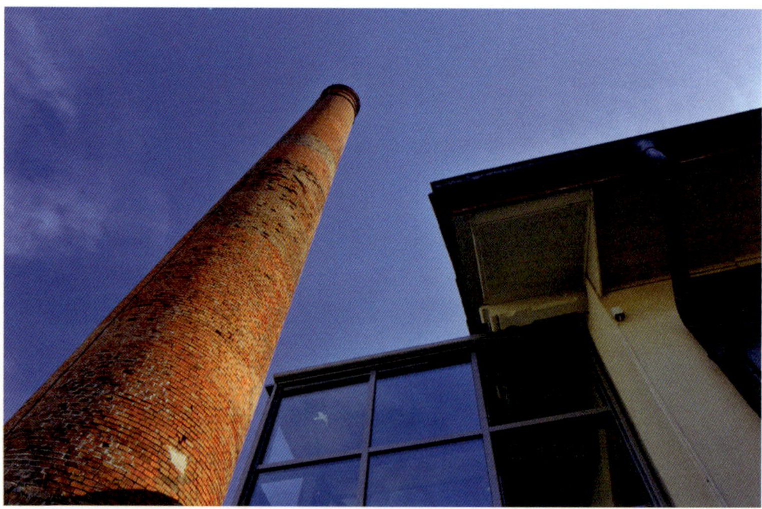

The extra-low viewpoint exaggerates the convergence of the verticals. It also accentuates the contrast between old and new.

One way around this is to try and find a more distant and higher viewpoint – a balcony across the street, a bridge or a hillside. Another approach is to accept that your verticals are going to converge and go with it. Lie down at the base of the building with a wide angle lens and exaggerate the effect.

Private property

Inside most buildings, including churches, you will be on private property. Check to see if photography is allowed. In some places hand-holding your camera is okay, but using a tripod is forbidden. Either seek permission (you may have to pay a fee), or you could try using a monopod. People don't seem to notice them so much.

Another way to get long exposures is to place your camera on a bench or wall, propped up with your bean bag.

Keys to the zoo

Some photography guides suggest that, if you're in a zoo with bars on the cages, you can photograph the animals successfully by getting up as close to the bars as possible so that they blur beyond recognition. Unfortunately, no matter how close you get there will always be some degree of distortion. It's like looking through dirty glasses. Also, being so close, there's the danger that you'll find a bit of your camera or, worse still, a bit of yourself inside the cage.

Instead, choose a zoo where moats or ditches are used to separate humans and animals, and use your telephoto lens, with a tripod or beanbag. Or, if there is no alternative, choose a high vantage point so that you are looking down. There is almost always a solution if you look around.

QUICK T!P

If you want to remember the details about the animals in a zoo, take a photograph of the information sign as well. To save on memory you can set your camera to its lowest quality for these shots.

Getting close up and personal

Getting really, really close is called macro photography. It can enable you to produce some stunning and unusual images of everyday things such as flowers, rocks and household items. True macro photography means capturing a life-sized image in your camera. It is a highly specialized field with its own techniques and equipment and you will need a lens that will focus very, very close to the subject. Unfortunately, most ordinary lenses will not focus closer than about a meter or so.

However, there are ways in which you can dip your toe in the macro waters. For example, your camera may have a 'closeup' mode. If it doesn't you could take a photograph from as close as your camera will allow and then enlarge the relevant bit. You can also buy supplementary lenses which fit in front of your lens and magnify the image.

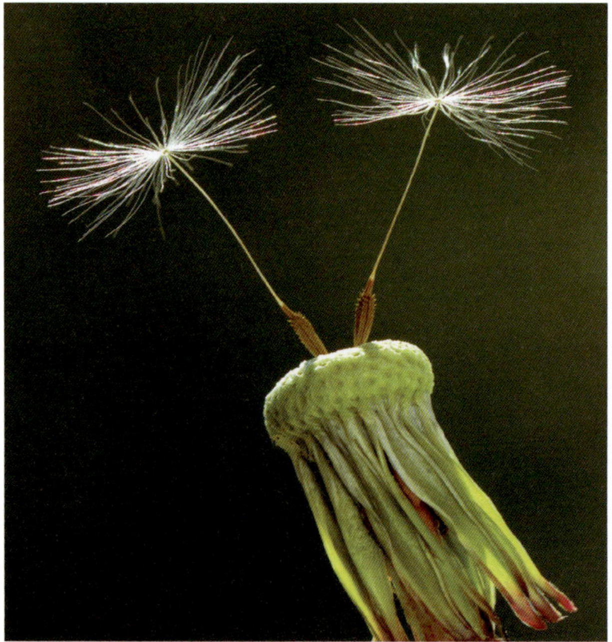

Getting super-close can transform the everyday to the intriguing.

Be a little backward

There are more options for close-up photography if you have a camera with interchangeable lenses. One of the cheapest ways is by reversing the lens. That's right … putting it on the camera backwards. You can buy a special adaptor which will enable you to do this (it's called, unsurprisingly, a 'reversing ring'). But this method will not work with all lenses, so test yours first by holding it in place manually while you take a few experimental shots.

With the simplest and cheapest reversing rings you will lose all the automatic features of your lens. More expensive ones have additional bits and bobs which will still allow them to be used, even though the lens is on backwards.

Extending your reach

However, if you want to get serious in the field of close-up photography you will need to think about getting a set of extension tubes, bellows, or even a true macro lens.

Extension tubes and bellows simply fit between the lens and the camera, allowing you to wind the lens further and further away. The further away the lens is, the closer it focuses. There is no extra glass in these accessories, so image quality does not suffer, but the image becomes dimmer and dimmer as the lens is moved away from the camera.

The other alternative is to get a true macro lens. This is a lens that will record the subject on the image sensor at the same size as it is in real life. This is known as a 1:1 reproduction ratio.

Giving specific tips on how to use this equipment is beyond the scope of this book. Check the appendix for websites giving additional information.

QUICK T!P

Getting close exaggerates camera shake, so use a tripod.

Spray-hey!

If you're taking close-up pictures of flowers or fruit, give them a few bursts with a water-spray bottle (the sort of thing used when ironing clothes) to create a little artificial dew. It freshens up an image beautifully. Just don't overdo it. You don't want to drown your subject, and too much dew looks false.

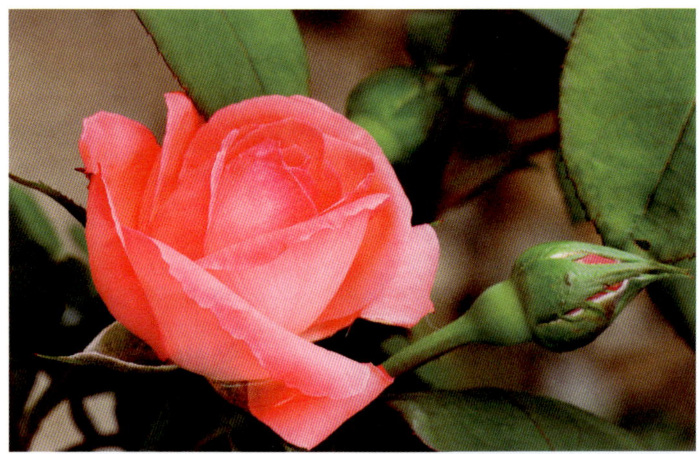

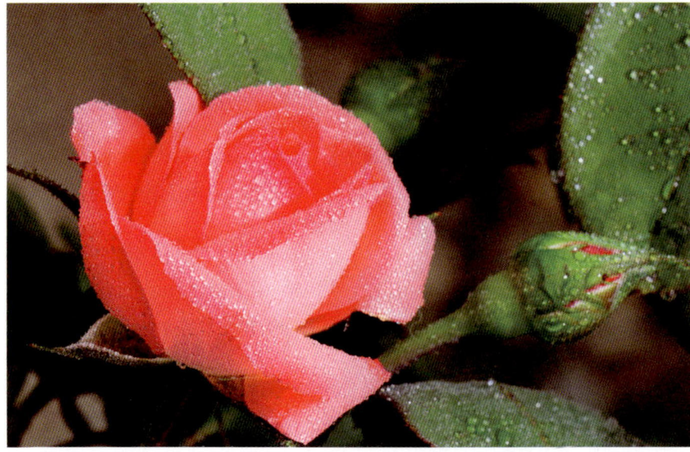

A few bursts with a water spray freshens this rose.

Thunderstruck?

How do photographers get those amazing shots of lightning zapping down from storm clouds?

This is one area in which digital cameras excel because, if you try this, you'll end up with an awful lot of blank shots. But you don't need to be lightning-fast with your shutter finger.

It can only be done when lightning strikes at night. Have a piece of black card ready. Put your camera on a secure tripod pointing at the approaching storm with the lens at its wide-angle setting. Switch off the autofocus and focus on infinity. Use manual exposure. Set the shutter speed either to 'bulb' (when the shutter remains open as long as you press the button) or to the slowest shutter speed you have. Choose an aperture of $f8$ for starters, though you will need to experiment with this. For example, if there are streetlights reflected off the clouds a smaller aperture may work

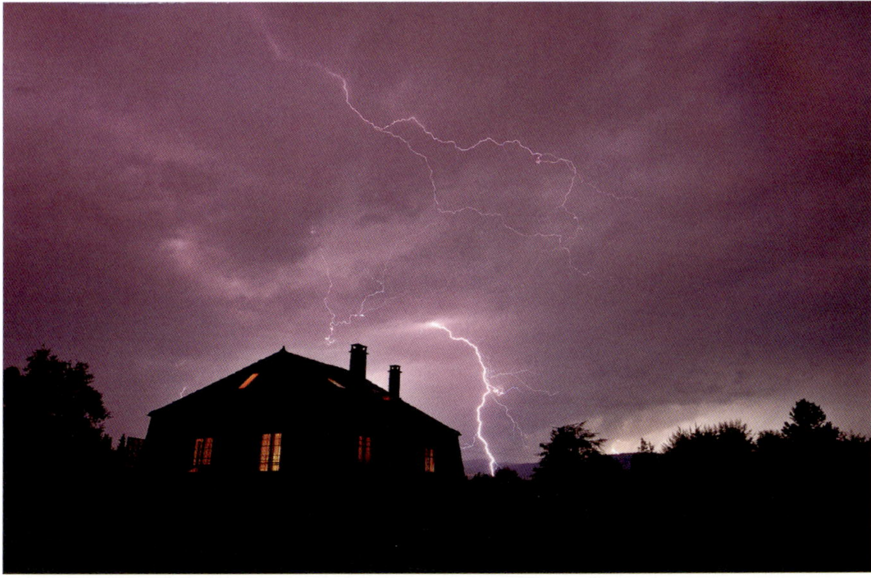

If it gets too close, high-tail it inside!

better. On the other hand, if it is very dark you'll have to open the aperture. You want a bit of surrounding detail to register, such as trees or buildings, because a lightning flash by itself doesn't look like much.

When the storm gets close enough, press the shutter release. If there is a lightning flash whilst the shutter is open, cover the lens with the black card until it closes again. This stops too much light getting in through the lens, or a secondary flash spoiling the first one.

Continue taking long-exposure pictures until the storm dies away or gets dangerously close. But don't take any risks. Tripods are usually made of metal! If the lightning starts striking too close, pack up, retreat to a place of safety and examine the results. If you've caught a strike, it will be dramatic.

There'll be fireworks

Firework photography is similar to lightning photography, except fireworks are more predictable. You also need to consider wind direction. Fireworks make smoke. If you get downwind it can obscure your pictures.

Set your camera up on a tripod and use a shutter speed that is long enough to capture the full sequence of a firework. For example, if you are shooting rockets, open the shutter as it is launched (to get the trail) and then close the shutter (or cover the lens) when the burst has died away. Two to five seconds should do it. You'll need to experiment with the aperture setting, but start with f8 again. Don't think that, because you're taking photos in the dark, you need the widest setting. You're taking pictures of the bursts, not the sky. The best aperture will depend on the power of the fireworks and how close you are to them. As you take shots of different fireworks try varying the aperture, so that at least some will come out perfectly exposed.

QUICK T!P

Fireworks go up. So the vertical (portrait) format is generally best.

Opposite: Taken with a 35mm lens, set at f8 and an exposure of 2 seconds. The trees, silhouetted in the foreground, add some depth to this image.

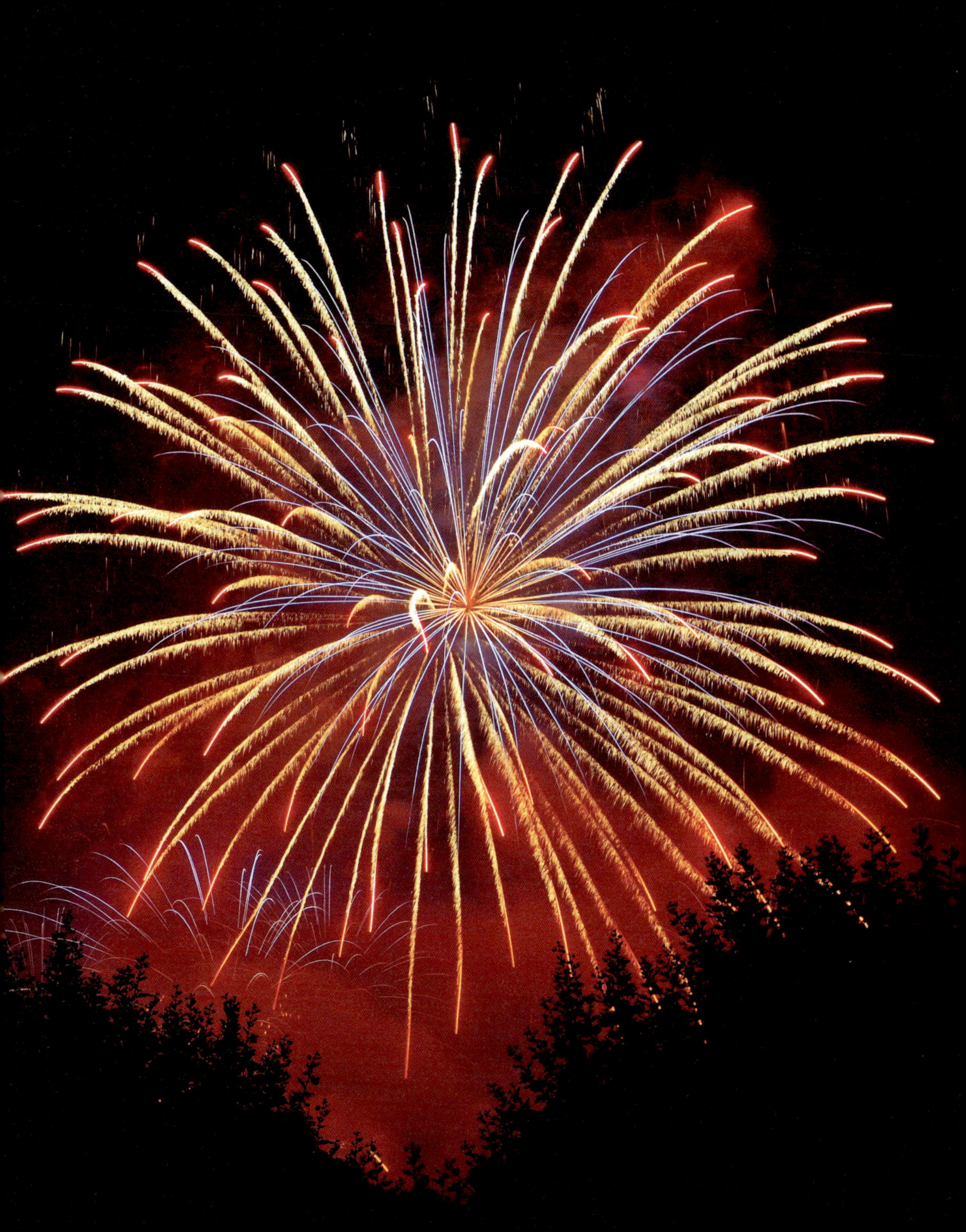

Water, water everywhere

Water is all around us, in fountains, puddles, ponds, lakes. Include it in your images wherever possible to add sparkle. In particular, when photographing something on or beside water, don't forget to include its reflection. Reflections can turn an ordinary picture into a great one.

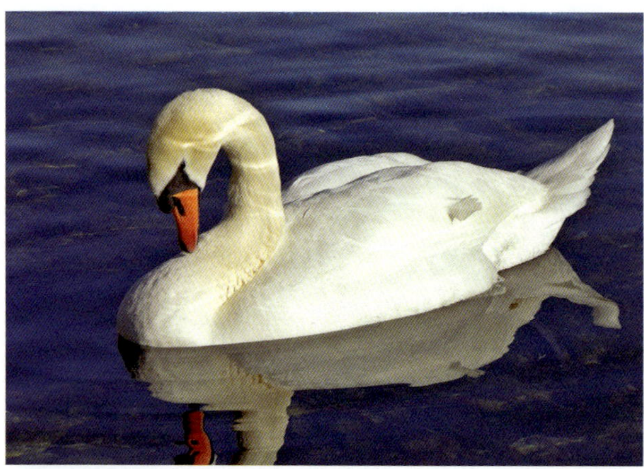

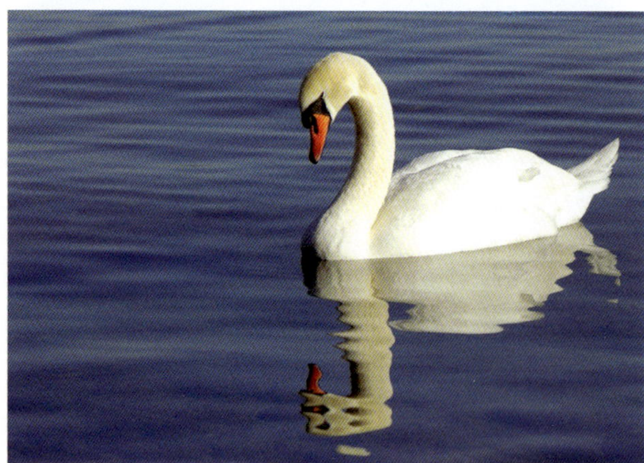

Top: Homing in …

Bottom: … or pulling back to include the full reflection.

Which gives the more interesting image?

Leave it out

You can also experiment by photographing just the reflection of something. Leave out the object that is being reflected, and flip the image by 180 degrees when you're doing the processing. This technique can produce some eye-catching abstract images.

Absolutely abstract

More arresting abstract images can be produced from all sorts of everyday objects and materials – rocks, grass, tiles, fabrics, ice crystals, even drain covers. The trick is to see them in a new and different way. Look for strong patterns, subtle colors or attractive textures. Low lighting often helps to bring out these elements. Try to include some perspective to give the image depth.

Another approach is to use blur to emphasize pattern and texture. For example, try this. Place your camera on a tripod and set it to a relatively long shutter speed, say 1 second. Then zoom in on a subject while the shutter is open. Just make sure that the subject – a person, for example, or someone's face – is in the center of the image. Otherwise it will be blurred beyond recognition.

And remember, if you are deliberately blurring an image, try to keep at least one small part of it relatively sharp. Images that are blurred all over look like mistakes.

Wave your magic wand

Did you know you can use a hand torch to 'paint with light'? Using it like a magic wand you can get some remarkable images. Here's what you do:

Your subject, whether it is big or small, should be in almost complete darkness. Set up your camera on a tripod, focus and stop the lens right down to a small aperture so you have a long exposure time. Take a preliminary shot without using your 'wand' to check that there are no stray light sources to pollute your image. (You'd be surprised how light the night can be.) Then take the 'real' picture. While the shutter is open, play your torch over the parts of the subject you want illuminated. Holding it still will give hard-edged spots of light, waving it about will make the light more diffuse. Keep doing this until you hear the shutter close.

You will probably have to experiment with exposure times, and the amount you 'paint' with your torch, in order to get things right. But that's the beauty of digital photography. You can experiment all you want, it costs nothing, you can see the results immediately, and erase the duds.

Another approach is to take pictures of people waving laser pointers or fireworks, maybe writing words with them, too. The principles, and techniques, are the same, but instead of using the light source to illuminate the photograph, you are actually photographing the light source itself.

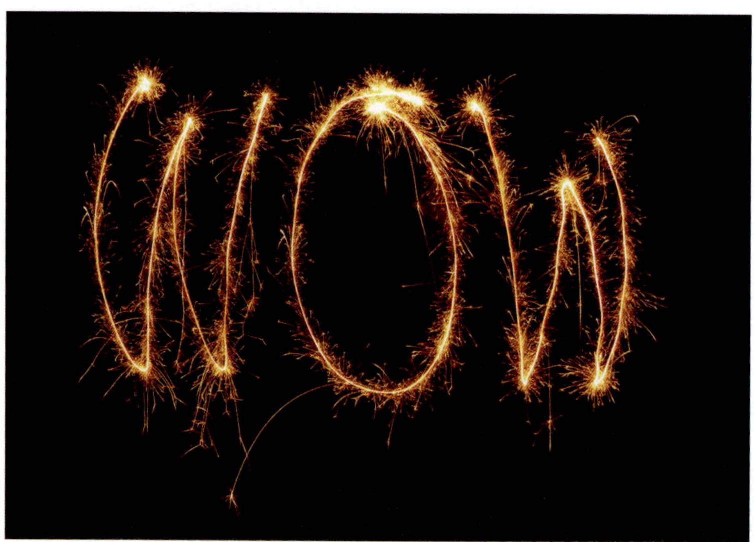

Wow! This was taken in one long exposure (15 seconds at f8) divided into three periods by briefly covering the lens with a piece of black card between drawing letters, to separate them.

Whatever you do, you will end up with some eye-catching images.

Silhouettes

Silhouettes, against vivid backgrounds, make powerful images. Here's how to take them:

Choose something that will be immediately recognizable as your subject, and make sure it is against a light background. Some of the best opportunities for silhouettes occur at sunrise and sunset, against the sky.

Set your camera exposure meter in spot mode, where it measures a single point, and take an exposure reading from the sky. You want it to be correctly exposed and the subject to be totally black. Then lock that exposure (or set it in manual) and fire away.

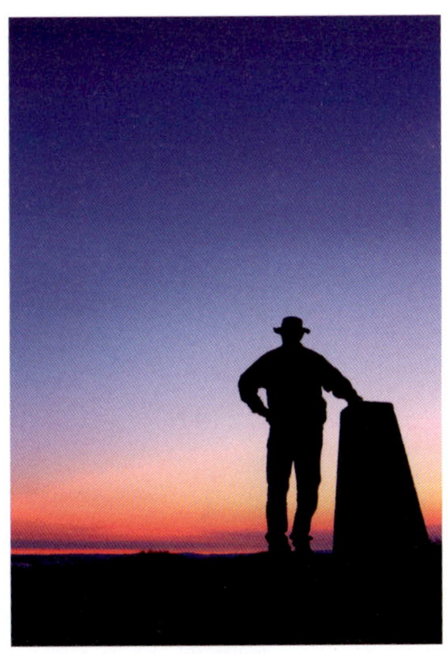

An hour or so before dawn (if you can get up!) is a good time for silhouettes. The sky is not too bright and has a beautiful color.

Keep them apart

Keep objects separate in a silhouette. For example, don't let your subject lean against a tree. Tree and person will merge into one mysterious shape. Also try to get people to pose in profile rather than looking straight on. That way their nose, mouth and eyes are outlined making them more recognizable.

Reverse silhouette

How about reversing a silhouette, so your subject is entirely surrounded by black?

Do this at night, with a distant background that is completely unlit. The night sky is the best option, but a distant hedge or the wall of a building will work, too. Set your camera to manual with the flash switched on, and experiment with the aperture and shutter speed to get the correct exposure of your subject. As the flash won't illuminate the background, your subject should stand out on a field of black.

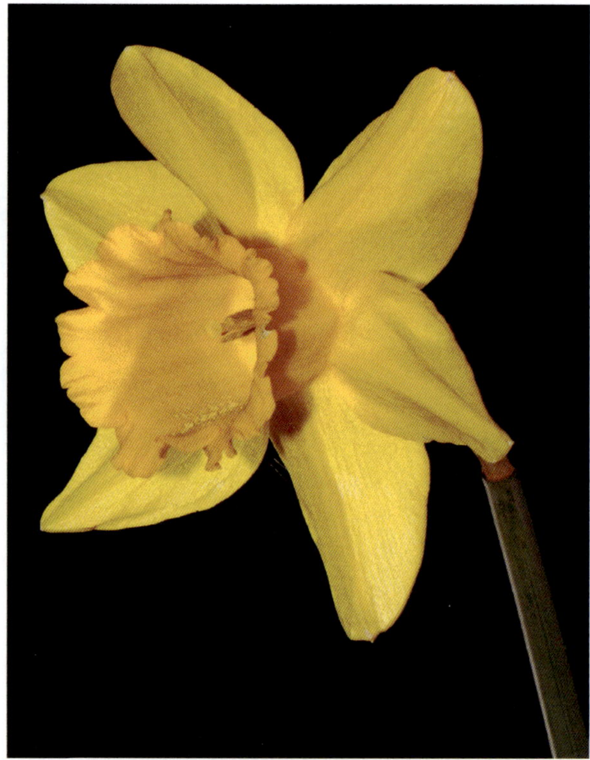

No special studio needed. This was taken against the night sky in my back garden.

Chapter summary

- When on holiday, take pictures that illustrate the destination, and others that tell a story.

- Look at postcards and brochures to get ideas for photographs, but then try to find a different viewpoint.

- Be careful when photographing people you don't know. Ask their permission and be aware of local laws.

- To photograph parades, find a spot near the start and choose a high viewpoint.

- Watch out for converging verticals when photographing buildings. Either exaggerate them, or find a high viewpoint.

- In zoos, try to find a spot where there are no bars in the way.

- Ultra-close-up photography can open up a whole new world in everyday places.

- To photograph lightning or fireworks, use a long shutter speed.

- Include water in your images to add sparkle. And don't forget the reflections.

- Try abstract photography, painting with light, or silhouettes.

> *You push the button –
we do the rest.*

1888 slogan for Kodak Photograph Company

Take Care

Chapter 10

Take Care

Having bought your super-duper camera you will probably want to look after it. There is not a lot that needs doing. The principal maintenance activity is keeping it clean, and most of that cleaning is external. Here's how to do it …

It's in the bag

You can reduce the need for cleaning, in the first place, by keeping your camera in a case or a bag when it's not in use. Not only will this help to keep the dust off, but most bags are padded too, protecting your camera if you drop it.

Don't advertise

If you have a lot of expensive equipment, lenses and the like, avoid buying a flashy bag with the manufacturer's name emblazoned on it. All this does is tell potential thieves, "Here are some valuable goodies to steal." Many professional photographers carry their cameras, lenses and other equipment in beat-up old bags. Apparently one top fashion photographer used to arrive at shoots with his equipment in an old shopping bag.

Essentials

When you come to clean your camera the main items you'll need are:

1. A soft lens brush.

2. A rocket blower. This is a big, egg-sized rubber bulb with a plastic nozzle at one end. Don't bother with those tiddly blowers that are combined with a brush. They're little better than useless.

3. A microfiber cleaning cloth, and lens cleaning tissues. Best to have both as they have different uses. If you only get one, get the cloth.

4. A kit for cleaning the sensor (see below).

A major dust-up

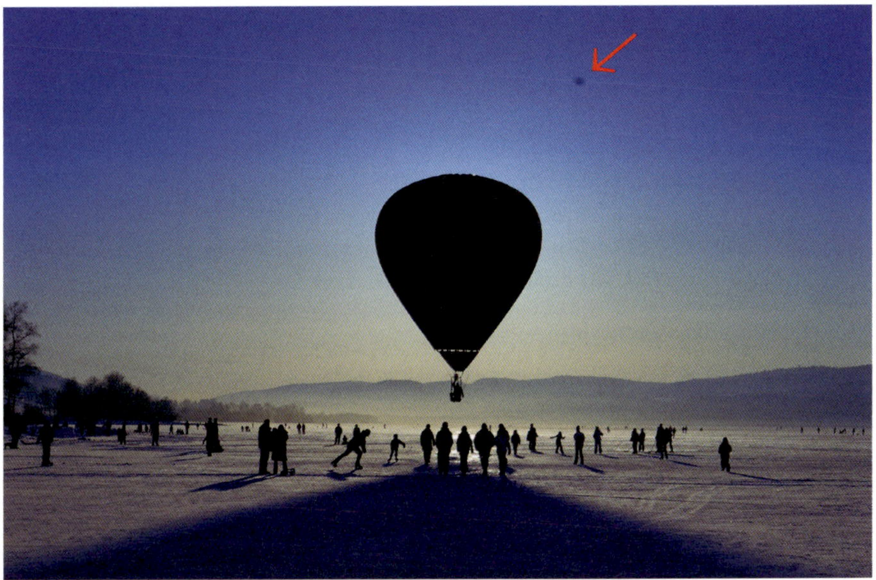

Is it a bird? Is it a plane? No, it's a dust-spot. Don't worry, it can be 'cloned out' with image-editing software.

One of the big headaches of digital single lens reflex cameras is dust on the sensor. Actually, it's not the sensor that gets dust on … it's an anti-aliasing and IR block filter that's placed over the sensor. But that's academic. The result is the same. You get fuzzy spots on your images, particularly visible in large areas of plain color like the sky. You can minimize the problem by:

1. Switching off the camera before changing lenses. When switched on the sensor has a electric current running through it that may attract dust.

2. Pointing the camera body downwards as you take the lens off. Dust tends to fall down and if you point the camera up it will act like a dust trap.

3. Putting the new lens on before you pack the old lens away. This closes the camera body as quickly as possible.

4. Being careful where you change your lens. It's not a good idea if you're standing in a windy, dusty street.

Clean up your act

Many DSLR cameras now have anti-dust devices built in, such as vibrating sensors. Whilst these work well, they are not the definitive answer. You are still likely to get dust stuck to your sensor at some stage. And when you do, there are various methods for removing it. They run through four steps, of increasing complexity.

Before you begin, choose a dust-free area with still air, lock up the mirror, remove the lens and …

a. Blow it off with a blast of air.

Use the rocket blower for this, with the camera held upside down. As you blow be careful not to let the plastic tip of the blower strike the lens mounting flange as tiny chips of plastic may break off, adding to the dust. Canned compressed air is unsuitable because the cans sometime spit out gobs of propellant, which is not good for the sensor.

However, be aware that this first step may not be very effective if you have a vibrating sensor. The vibrations generally have the same effect as the air-blast, and if they haven't shifted the dust it is unlikely that the blower will.

b. Wipe it off with a statically-charged brush.

This is a fine-haired brush, with an electric spinner to 'charge' it. Having charged the bristles you then wipe the brush across the sensor to lift off any dust. But don't touch the brush hairs with your fingers or you will be transferring finger-grease to the sensor.

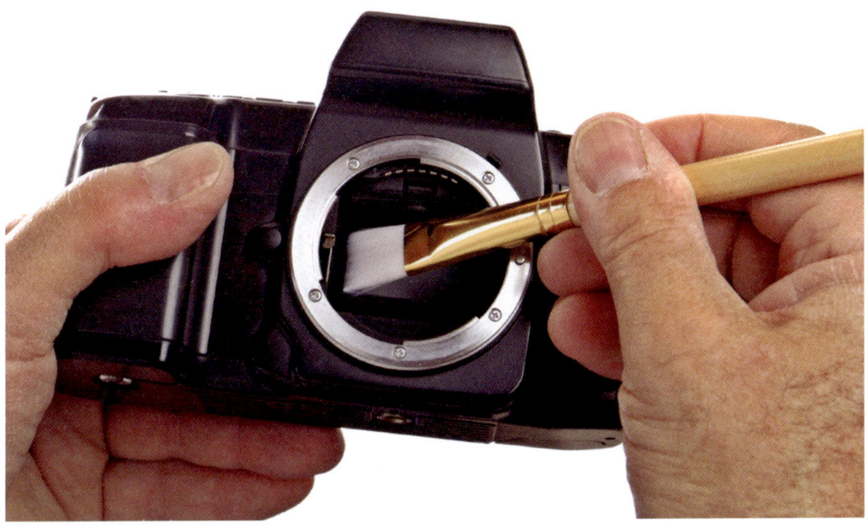

Despite warnings in the manual, you can clean your camera sensor if you're careful. Here it is being done with a statically-charged brush.

c.   Wipe it off using a kit with special swabs and cleaning fluid.

You apply a drop of the cleaning fluid to a spatula-shaped swab and stroke it lightly across the sensor. This method works best for dust that is 'welded' on and can't be removed by the previous two methods.

d.   Or, ignore the previous three steps, don't do anything at all, and take the camera back to the dealers who will offer a cleaning service.

QUICK T!P

The bathroom is one of the best places for cleaning the sensor as it is usually the most dust-free room in the house. The shower and other falling water helps remove dust from the air.

Which is best?

That depends on your nerves. If you're frightened by the awful warnings in some camera instruction manuals, avoid the three do-it-yourself methods and go to the dealer. But, be warned, it will work out very expensive and you'll be without your camera for a while.

As for the other three methods, no one is best. They all remove the dust in different ways and should be regarded as a sequence. First use the blower/vibration method. Then check for dust (see 'Dust dismay', below, for how to do this). If there are still stubborn spots, use the static brush method, and check again. If there are *still* dust spots after that, try to swab them off.

And if that hasn't got rid of everything, and it is really bugging you, then take the camera back to the dealer for professional cleaning.

Just don't ever use another method sometimes advocated on the internet – placing a piece of sticky tape on the sensor, sticky side down, and peeling it off again to lift off the dust. I blanch at the thought of what *that* leaves behind.

Dust dismay

If you want to check how much dust there is on your sensor – before and after cleaning, for example – there is a very simple way to do it. But, be warned, this will show up every, but *every*, last speck. So it's not for the faint-hearted.

Mount your lens with the smallest aperture on the camera, use the aperture-priority mode, and turn down to that smallest setting.

Point your camera at a clear sky, or a blank white wall, and take a photograph. Don't worry if, the shutter speed is way too slow for hand-holding (because you are using such a small aperture). That doesn't matter. You're not taking a photograph of anything external. The dust moves with the camera.

Download the blank image to your computer, and look at it on the screen. It won't be blank! You will probably see dust spots everywhere, particularly around the edges.

But don't get neurotic

Accept the fact that, whatever you do with a DSLR, you're going to get dust on your sensor. Every time you operate the shutter, its gears and levers wear a fraction, producing minute particles. Then you need to change lenses from time to time. And even if you don't ever change lenses, your zoom lens will probably act like an air pump. Whenever you zoom in and out it will draw air, and dust, into and out of the camera body.

Most of the gunk can be removed. And if an image is spoiled by dust spots you can always 'clone' them out using an image editing program.

Lens cleaning

Inevitably you are going to get dust and smears on the outside of your lens, too. Don't clean them off with the tail of your shirt or your handkerchief. Of course, you wouldn't do a thing like that, would you? But you would be surprised by how many people do.

Most lenses have a delicate anti-reflective coating on them, so use the blower to remove any particles that may be abrasive. Place a drop of lens cleaning fluid on to your lens cloth (or tissue) and wipe the lens clean with a circular motion. Don't wipe too hard on the lens as you can wear away the special coatings. Use the blower to dry the lens, or let it dry naturally.

Watch out you don't create a 'worn spot' by cleaning your lens the same way each time. Alternate the circular motion with up and down or sideways movements.

What a contrast!

The effects of dust on the sensor of your camera are easy to spot … they're spots … and they can be relatively easily 'cloned out' with image-editing software.

The effects of dust on the lens are far more insidious. They will not show up as spots no matter how big the dust specks are. Instead, dust on the lens reduces contrast and sharpness, and muddies colors. These effects are almost impossible to correct with your image-editing program, so make sure your lens is squeaky-clean before you start.

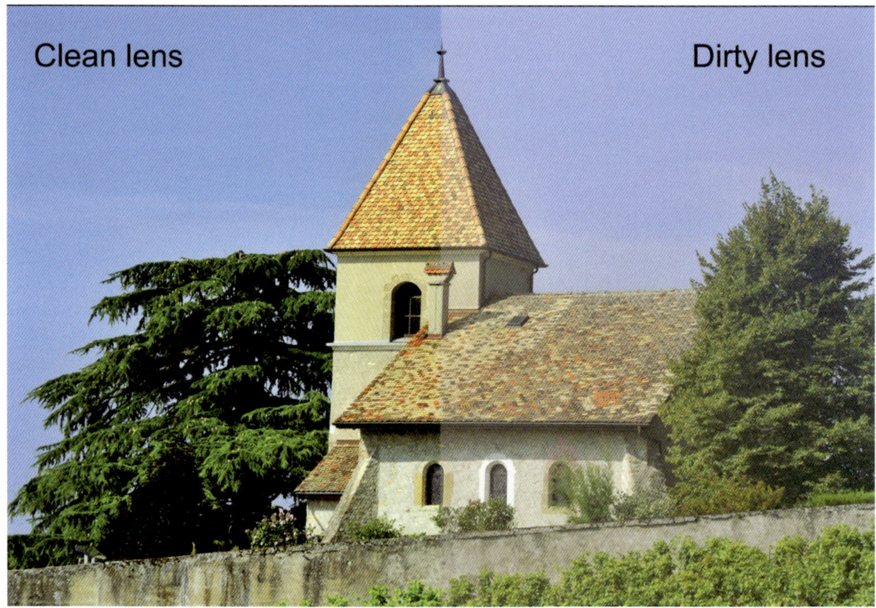

Dirt on the surfaces of the lens will cause loss on contrast and washed-out colors.

And keep it clean by replacing the lens cap every time you stop shooting.

Protection racket

One simple way to protect your lens is to buy an ultra violet (UV) or 'skylight' filter and keep it screwed on to the front permanently. Although these filters appear to be clear sheets of glass that cost the earth, they will seal the lens surface without having any effect on exposure times, or changing the colors of a scene.

You can take a filter off to clean it. And if you have an accident what's better – a broken filter or a broken lens? In addition, it will reduce haze if you are shooting landscapes.

Cooling off period

If you're photographing outside on a winter's day your camera is going to get cold. Not only does this affect the capacity of the batteries (see 'Cold comfort', below) but, more seriously, when you return to the warmth inside, condensation is going to form on the camera and lens. A little bit of moisture on the exterior is no big deal. But if water condenses inside the camera body, or between the lens elements, it can have serious effects. Electronic circuitry can malfunction, dust particles on the sensor can become 'welded' in place by the moisture, and condensation between the lens elements can be difficult to eliminate.

Play safe and, before coming in to the warmth, put your camera in a plastic bag, expel as much air as possible and seal the bag. Only take it out when all the equipment has warmed up to room temperature.

Battery and assault

There you are, watching grandpa reeling in the biggest catch of his fishing career. You raise your camera, press the shutter and … nothing happens.

The batteries are dead.

No. It's no use assaulting your camera. Buy spare batteries, make sure they're fully charged and always have them with you. It doesn't matter how good your camera is. With flat batteries it's just an inert lump of metal and glass.

Cold comfort

Cold weather reduces the power of your camera's batteries. If you're desperate, it's cold, and your batteries run flat, you can sometimes coax enough energy out of them for a shot or two more by putting them in your pocket to warm up for a while. But don't rely on this! Start a cold winter's shooting session with fully-charged batteries.

Play your cards right

As well as having a spare set of batteries, you should also carry at least one spare memory card. When that perfect photo opportunity presents itself, the last thing you want to be doing is sorting through the images on a full card, erasing the ones that you don't want in order to make space.

Keep your cards cool and dry, preferably in their protective cases, and keep them well away from strong magnetic sources such as audio speakers. Or you can buy dedicated memory-card carrying cases that will take several cards at once and protect them. These cases are well worth their modest cost.

It's too filling

Don't fill your memory card completely full. Because of the way in which cards store files, that last picture, which fills it completely, can corrupt the whole thing. Always try to leave space for at least one image.

And, if you have a series of irreplaceable photos and you want to be super-cautious, don't fill the card more than 80% full.

Chapter summary

- Put together a camera care kit.

- Dust on the sensor is a problem with DSLR cameras. But it is inevitable. Don't worry about it.

- Reduce the amount of dust that collects by changing lenses carefully.

- Only clean your camera's sensor, or the lens, when it is needed.

- To clean your sensor use a blast of air, static-charged brush or special cleaning fluid only. Or have it done professionally. Do not use 'home remedies'.

- Clean your lens with a microfiber cloth and lens cleaning fluid.

- Reduce the need for lens cleaning by using a clear UV filter.

- Carry at least one extra, fully-charged battery.

- Carry several spare memory cards. They are not harmed by airport x-ray machines.

- Don't fill your memory card completely full.

"Good photographers work hard to find their own style, their own groove, and everybody should strive towards that."

Lisa Gagne – Top-selling stock photographer

Cash from
Your Camera

Chapter 11
Cash from Your Camera

Yes, you can earn interesting money from your hobby. It is fun, challenging and can be satisfying. But don't let anyone tell you it is easy.

First of all, you've got to have the gear for it. Standards and technical requirements in commercial photography are high and, unless you happen to be present at a major newsworthy incident, forget about taking pictures with a little compact. At the minimum you will need a camera capable of taking pictures at a resolution of 300 dots per inch, and 6 megapixels in size.

It is better, if you are intending to work at this level, to go for a DSLR camera and to have a range of lenses to cover various situations.

Beyond that, it is all about meeting the needs of the customer, whether that person is a neighbor wanting a portrait, or an agency with a commission to fill. Here are some ideas …

Be in it to win it!

You can win big in competitions but the rules are important, especially the ones in small print. A surprising number of people don't read them and are disqualified. That wouldn't be you, would it?

Beyond that, research the competition in as much detail as you can. Look at the previous year's winners, not only to get an insight into what the judges are looking for, but also to avoid submitting the same sort of thing again.

Opposite: Taken with a film camera, this image has won me awards in national and international competitions.

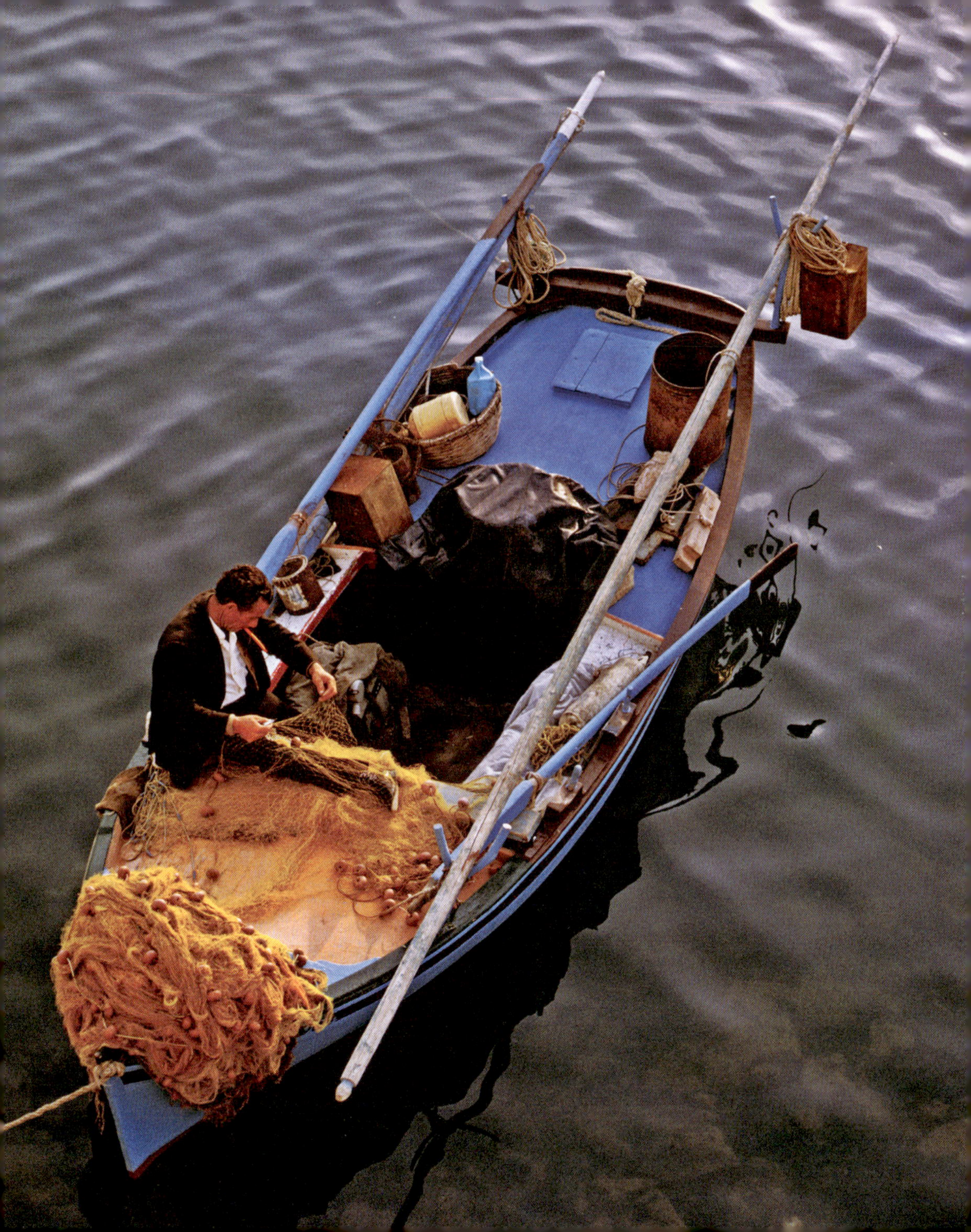

Then, to produce a winning image, think hard. It may be best to abandon the first idea you have. Dozens of people will probably think of the same thing. Be original, and try to photograph something specifically rather than relying on an existing image. What's more, it goes without saying that your image must be perfectly exposed, well-composed and pin-sharp. Be super-critical. If you have the slightest doubt as to whether it's good enough, reject it and try again.

All rights not all right!

Carefully read the terms and conditions of any competition. If they state that the organizers take 'all rights' to all entries, stay away! This is called 'rights grabbing' and, by simply entering the competition, you are giving away your copyright. In other words, you no longer own the image you submit. Whether you win or not, if the company uses your photo in a big advertising campaign you get nothing.

A surprising number of competitions, some run by reputable companies, practice 'rights grabbing'. It's a quick and easy way for the organizers to boost their photo library.

Faking it

Beware of fake competitions. You can tell if you've entered one because you'll receive a gushing response telling you how great your photo is. The organizers will want to print it in a book with an impressive name, which you can buy at a vastly inflated price. Forget it. You, and all the others who have been taken in, will be the only ones to buy the book.

Calendars

There are two types of calendars that use photographs – retail and corporate.

Retail calendars are the sort that you buy in shops at Christmas. The photographs on those have almost all been taken by professionals, probably using large format cameras. It is a very difficult market to break in to. However, there are certain companies who are open to skilled amateurs and will send you their guidelines if you ask.

Corporate calendars sound grand (and some of them are) but there are also many produced for local businesses – a garage, restaurant or cab company. These frequently want good photographs of local sights. Often they want an image of their own business. You could try giving them a call. But don't do it in November. That's way too late. March is not too early to start making enquiries for the following year.

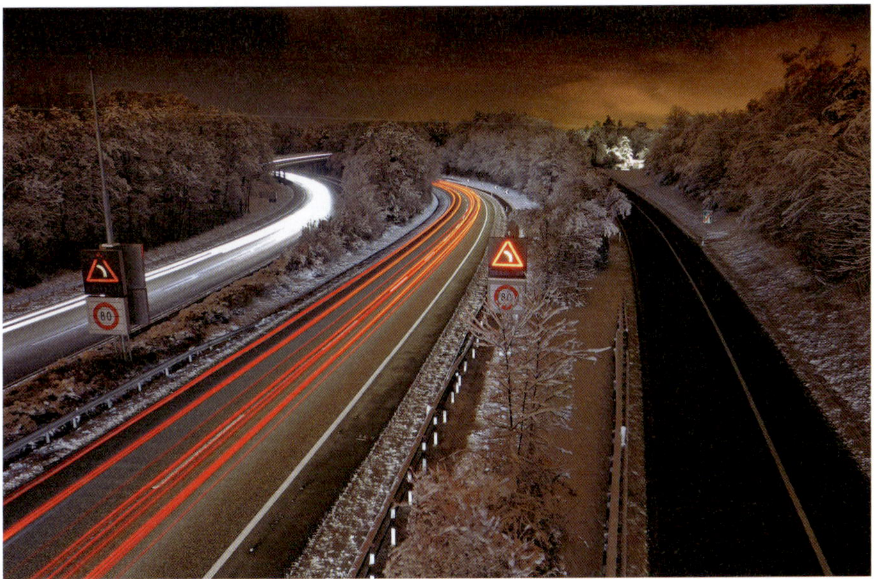

Your camera can reveal things in a new way. This long-exposure (30 seconds) was taken from a bridge over a freeway after a light fall of snow. It too has won me prizes in photographic competitions.

The other option is to make your own calendar and try to sell it. The problem with that is that you have to foot the bill yourself, and do all the marketing – a huge task. Some print-on-demand internet sites allow you to do this at minimal cost, and sell your calendar online. But, be warned, sales are usually not high. Be realistic, it's likely that the only people who will buy your own calendar will be family and friends.

You could also sell your self-produced calendar at local craft fairs and similar events. But, then, when will you get time for photography?

Postcards

Many of the retail calendar companies also produce postcards but, once again, it is a tough market. The majority of postcards are aimed at tourists who want pictures of historic buildings, cityscapes beauty spots, people practicing quaint customs and similar. Image quality has to be perfect, and the professionals who produce photographs for postcards are usually using large-format cameras.

As with calendars, you have the option of producing your own and selling them through shops, or at craft fairs and bazaars. There are a number of companies who will print small runs of postcards – say 1,000 – at reasonable prices, so the outlay is less than for printing your own calendars. Check in the back of photographic magazines for companies that provide this service.

However, as with self-produced calendars, marketing postcards is a time-consuming process.

Portrait photography

This can be a very lucrative field, but you need to build up a reputation to be successful.

Keep things simple at first. You don't need a lot of equipment to begin. Take portraits outside, or inside using window light and a reflector. Build up an initial portfolio, taking portraits of family and friends, giving them free prints in return. Use this portfolio to show new customers, and keep updating it as you get more and more commissions.

Wedding hells

Fancy spending your weekends trying to be invisible whilst surrounded by hundreds of people who are enjoying themselves? Spurred on by the challenge of photographing someone in pure white whilst her partner is in black? Enjoy herding cats?

Make no mistake, wedding photography is very stressful. But if you think you can handle it, then it can be a big money earner. And, on top of that, producing a beautiful album, that a couple will treasure for years to come, is highly satisfying.

However, you need to be professional, and there is absolutely no room for error. It's no good saying your camera battery has gone flat, and can they hold off with the nuptials whilst you recharge it.

Another important point to bear in mind is that the job won't just involve taking photographs. Sorting out the images back at your computer, selecting the best ones, cropping them, making the necessary adjustments, and similar work, will take a long time. On top of that, you need to find a good printer for the final images … and that doesn't mean the printer on your desk. Wedding photographs need to be of the highest quality. So find a reliable company, with top-class commercial equipment, who can meet deadlines.

Take stock

Stock photographs are generic images that designers use for advertisements, websites, books, reports, posters, programs. You name it, someone will need images for it. And buyers need a huge, and ever-growing, variety – everything from pictures of people to panoramas of mountains. You can sell your images through a variety of online agencies, all with slightly differing procedures. For most of them, you will be required to open a contributor account and submit some samples for initial approval.

Once you are approved you can send in photos as often as you wish (though some agencies do have upload limits). Every image is inspected for quality and commercial potential and, if accepted, is put up for sale. You may get a high rate of rejections, but don't let that put you off. Learn from the ones that are not accepted.

If you are ambitious you can sell the same photographs through several agencies. Remember, although the agencies are selling them, you still own the copyright. Never ever give away, or even sell, the copyright to your images (see 'For legal eagles', below).

Microstock

Microstock agencies operate online, selling images for low rates (from one dollar upwards). The photographer gets anything from 20% to 75% of the sale price. The rate varies from agency to agency depending on factors such as whether you are offering your photos exclusively, and how the buyer will use the image.

Twenty percent of one dollar may not sound a lot, but these agencies work on a "Pile 'em high, sell 'em cheap" philosophy, selling images over and over again, 24 hours a day, 7 days a week, throughout the world. Reasonably good photos may sell 20 or 30 times a month, and first-class ones over 100 times per month, over and over again. Also, $1 is the minimum price. Depending on the size of the image, or the way it's going to be used, prices can go up to $50 or more.

Macrostock

The principal difference between Micro and Macrostock agencies is the price at which they sell their images. Macrostock agencies are more like the traditional photographic agencies and sell images for hundreds of dollars upwards. The photographer's cut can be from 40% to 70% depending on the agency and their conditions.

If you have images with a macrostock agency, be aware that you are never going to sell any at a rate of 100, or even 20, per month. But when you do sell one, the money will be good.

The two 'V's

The key to a worthwhile income from stock photography is the two 'V's – 'volume' and 'variety'. Get a lot of photographs accepted by the agencies, on a whole range of different subjects. And keep submitting new material. In that way you build up a portfolio that sells and sells, even while you're asleep.

Stuck for ideas?

Wondering what to take photos of for the stock agencies? Look in magazines, newspapers and brochures. Note the sort of photographs that illustrate articles and advertisements. Cut out the ones that interest you and keep them in a file. Also jot down any ideas that occur to you and slip these notes into your file too.

Then, when you're stuck for inspiration leaf through your collection. Don't ever copy the images exactly, you could get into big and expensive trouble. But your 'scrapbook' will serve as inspiration from which you can create your own ideas.

The key to selling …

… is keywording. Buyers find images they want by using keywords such as 'businesswoman', 'success', 'family' 'Christmas', and so on.

With most agencies it is your job to add the keywords to your image. The better you can do this the more people will see your images, and the more they will sell.

A number of image editing programs allow you to attach keywords to images as you are processing them, which means you don't have to do it over and over again for each different agency.

Spam, spam, spam, spam, spam

Don't be tempted to indulge in 'keyword spamming'. That is, adding dozens of irrelevant ones in the hope that your image will pop up in all sorts of different searches and so be bought more often.

If you have a picture of a dog and you add the keywords such as 'cat', 'family', 'home', 'bone' (and, yes, people try this) your image will be rejected or, worse, you will be booted out of the agency completely.

Want a best-seller?

The best-selling stock photographs are those that include people, illustrate concepts, ideas or symbols, or tell a story. And if you can create a photograph that does all three you have a sure-fire winner.

It also helps if the image is simple, with a minimum of extraneous clutter, is eye-catching and does not become dated too quickly.

For legal eagles

The instant you take a photograph, you hold the copyright. You don't have to do anything to register it (though you can if you wish).

You are also entitled to license the photograph, that is sell (or give) someone the right to publish it according to agreed terms. Usually an agency does this for you – and takes a cut of the earnings.

Don't confuse copyright with exclusivity. Some agencies may ask you to place an image exclusively with them. That's fine. You still own the copyright, but you agree not to offer the image anywhere else and, as a result, you should get more money for it when it does sell.

Never sell your copyright or, worse, give it away in a 'rights grabbing' photo competition (see 'All rights not all right'). If you've done that, and the photo is a best-seller, you get nothing.

Read the Terms and Conditions of an agency carefully before you sign up with them. No reputable agency will take the copyright from you, and if one wants to, don't touch them with a bargepole.

Please release me

If you are taking pictures of people, they are recognizable, and you wish to sell the pictures for commercial purposes (as opposed to editorial – see below) then you must get your subjects to sign a model release. This is a legal document, signed by the subject of your photograph, stating that they give you full permission to sell their image.

A picture of a person for which you have a signed model release is far more saleable than one without.

A face in the crowd

"But I took photos at a parade and there are dozens of people in it. If I'm going to sell the image, do I need a model release for everyone?"

If the picture is going to be used for commercial purposes, such as advertising … yes, you do.

"Oh boy! That's impossible," you cry.

It is. That's why most 'crowd' scenes you see in advertisements will have been set up, using models.

Editorial

In the US and most of Europe, (and possibly in other countries too … but check) there is one exception to the model release requirement. As the law stands, you do not need model releases for people who appear in pictures published to illustrate a news story, an article in a magazine, newsletters, books or similar. This is called 'editorial' use.

A simple way of looking at it is that 'commercial use' involves selling, promoting or decorating a product that is sold for profit. 'Editorial use' is illustrating text.

However, this is not a clear-cut distinction and can sometimes be difficult to know if a use will be considered commercial or editorial. Play safe and get a model release if you can.

Private property

Be careful. If you take pictures on private land and you plan to sell them commercially, you will need a property release. Private land includes historical sites, shopping malls, railway and bus stations, airport terminals, parks, religious buildings and similar. You may have free access to a place, but that doesn't mean that it's public property. Sometimes there are notices about photography. More often there are not.

One thing you can be sure of is that if you've had to pay for access, you are on private property. You will probably see people taking photographs in such places, and wonder why no one is bothering them. Bear in mind that these photographs are being taken for private use, for example, as a memento of a family visit. It's a different kettle of fish if you are taking photographs in order to sell them.

Of course, you can always ask for the owner's permission. But, unfortunately, most owners are well aware of the commercial value of their property. They will usually ask for a hefty fee for signing a release, a fee that will usually swamp any income you may hope to make from the image.

FINAL T!P

After you've been using your camera for a while, read its manual again, carefully. It's amazing what hidden gems you can find in there.

Chapter summary

- If going in for competitions, read the rules.

- You stand more chance in local competitions than national ones.

- Good photographs are always needed for calendars and postcards.

- To get into portrait photography, build up a sample portfolio first.

- Wedding photography can be profitable, but it is also stressful. There's no room for mistakes.

- Stock photography agencies are always on the lookout for new material. But it has to be high quality.

- Volume and variety is the key to success with stock agencies … that and good keywording.

- Keep a file of photographs from newspapers and magazines to give you inspiration.

- The best-selling stock photographs are those that include people. But you'll need model releases.

- Get a property release if you're taking photographs on private land.

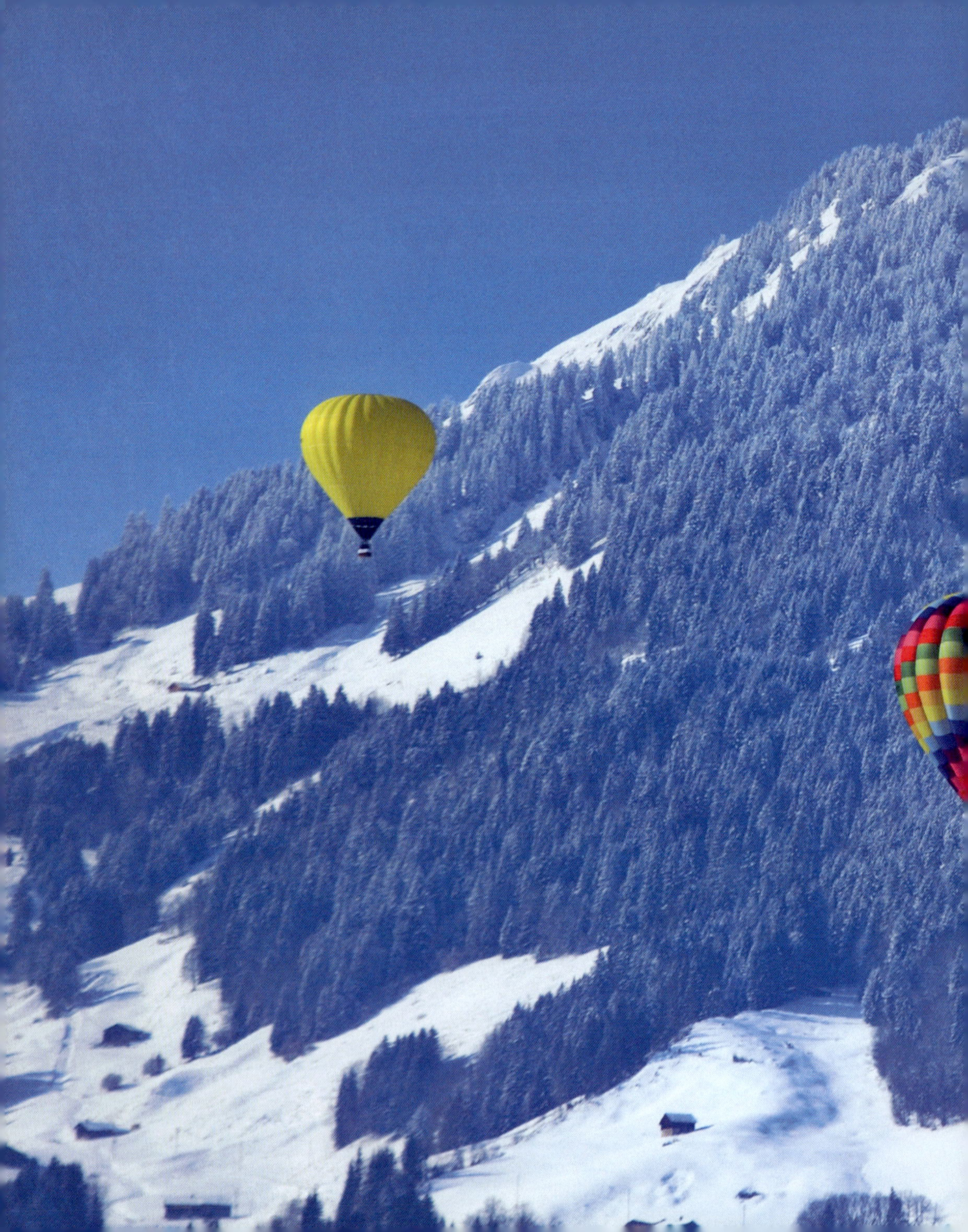

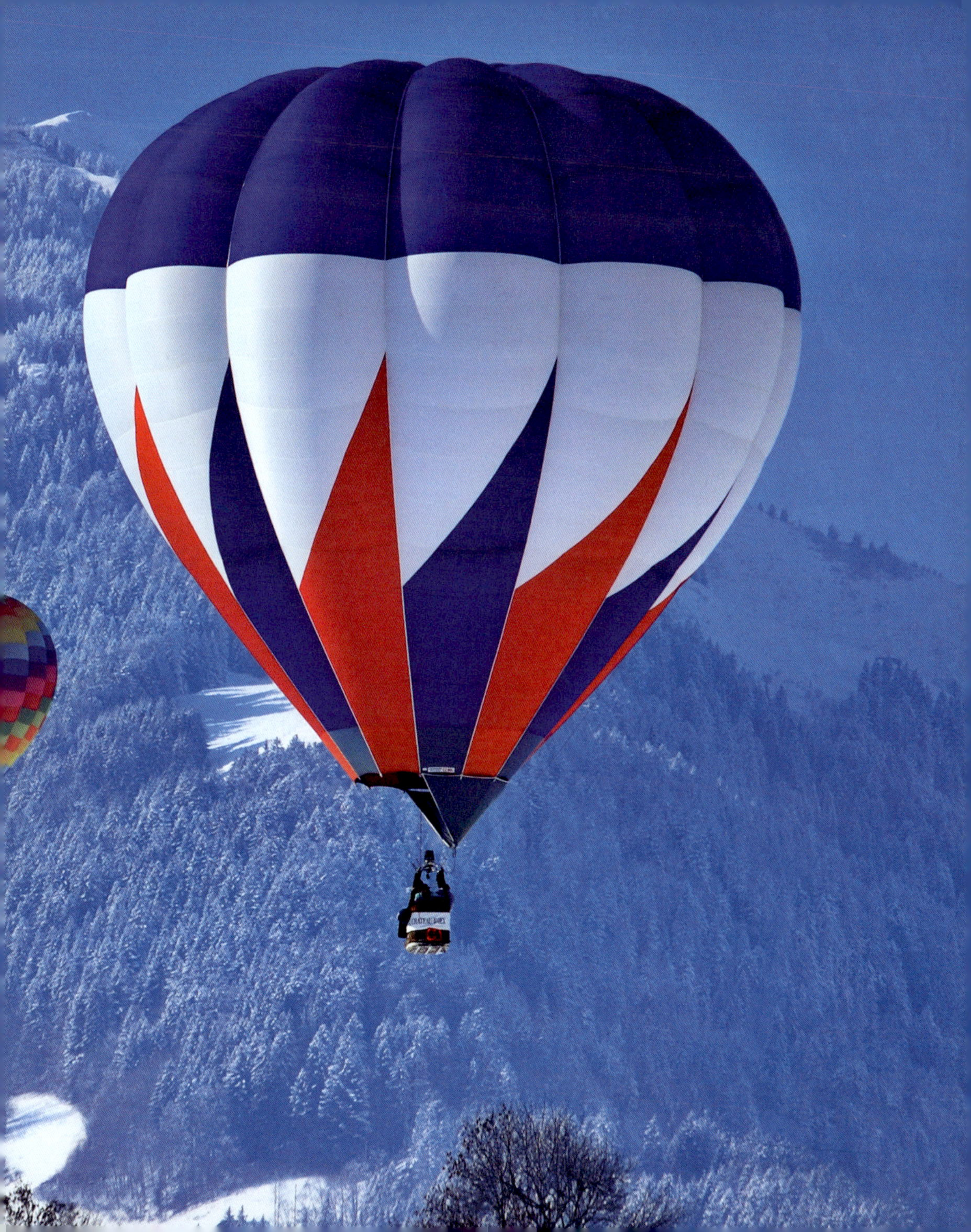

Appendix

Useful Websites

The PhotoZone

Alistair Scott's photo-blog – a mix of all things to do with photography, an up-to-date reference and source of photographic information.

http://www.alscotts.com

Heavens Above

Gives a wide range of astronomical data – sunrise and sunset times, moon phases, satellite passes across the sky, and more. You need to know where you are in the world in order to get accurate information but you can enter your location in a variety of ways, including the name of your town and country.

http://www.heavens-above.com

Sunrise sunset

Tells you sunrise and sunset times for any place on earth. You just have to put a pin in a map. It will also tell you, for your location, moonrise and moonset, the phase of the moon, and will produce a printable sunrise/sunset calendar for the whole year.

http://www.sunrisesunsetmap.com/

Dofmaster

All you need to know about depth of field including free programs for creating and printing calculators, and charts. These are particularly useful as many manufacturers no longer engrave depth of field scales on their lenses.

http://www.dofmaster.com

Microstock agencies

Below is a sample of microstock photo agencies that will sell your photographs for you. Photographs are sold for low prices, and the agency takes its commission, but a really good photograph can be a steady earner, selling over and over again. To become a contributing photographer you will need to apply with some sample images. Your submissions will be inspected and those that pass are put up on the agency's website. After you are accepted you can contribute whenever you like, though some agencies have uploading limits. You will have to do the keywording for your images.

iStock: http://www.istockphoto.com

Shutterstock: http://www.shutterstock.com/

Dreamstime: http://www.dreamstime.com/

Fotolia: http://us.fotolia.com/

Yay: http://yaymicro.com

A selection of freeware programs for photographers

The Photographer's Ephemeris

Shows you, on a map, where the sun and moon will rise and set on any date, at any place on earth. Is also available as a (paid-for) app for your phone. (Note: To install this program you also need another program called Adobe Air.)

http://photoephemeris.com/

Star trails

A freeware program that allows you to create amazing shots of star trails. You take a series of long-exposure night shots, one after the other, and then blend them together on your computer to give one image.

http://www.startrails.de/html/software.html

Stellarium

Like having a planetarium on your computer. Shows the sky, just as you would see it with stars, planets, moon and sun in real time. Or you can set it to show the sky any other time or date.

http://www.stellarium.org/

Hugin panorama stitcher

An open source, freeware program that allows you to assemble photographs into a complete panorama.

http://hugin.sourceforge.net/

Faststone

A free image viewer and sorter that also allows you to do a certain amount of editing. You can tag photos, view them at full size or larger, read the EXIF information for an image (that's the shooting data) and even look at the histogram.

http://www.faststone.org/

Visipics

When you're running out of disk space on your computer, this is a quick and easy-to-use program that finds all your duplicate images and allows you to delete them.

http://www.visipics.info

The Gimp

The mother of all freeware image editing programs, and a versatile graphics manipulation package as well. This is the free equivalent of Photoshop, and is nearly as good. It is open source software and so is constantly being updated.

http://www.gimp.org/